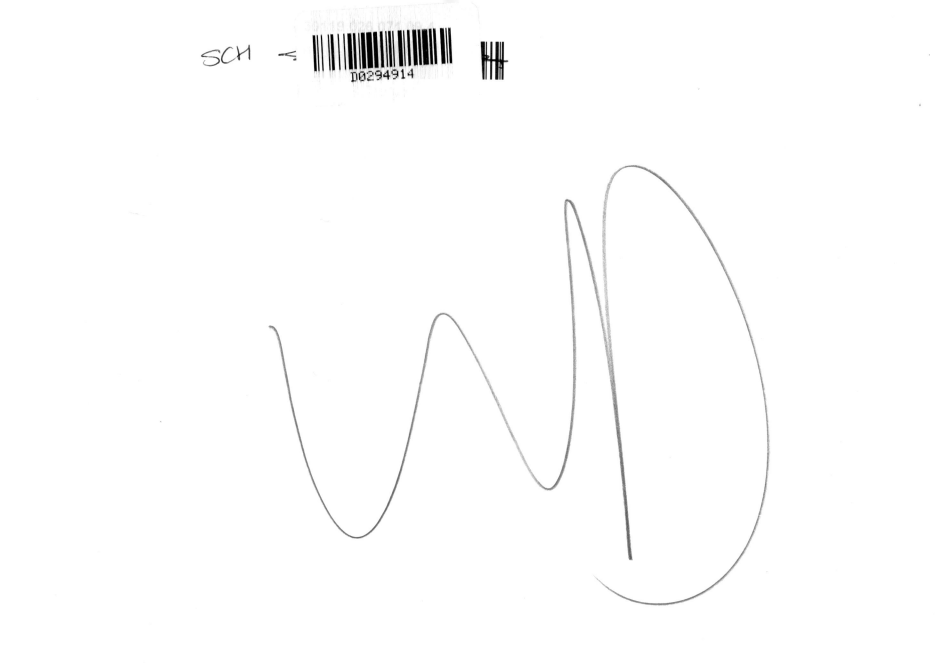

Michael H. C. Baker

STEAM ON THE WESTERN

The Final Decades

Ian Allan
PUBLISHING

First published 2010

ISBN 978 0 7110 3492 1

Published by Ian Allan Publishing

an imprint of Ian Allan Publishing Ltd, Hersham, Surrey, KT12 4RG
Printed in England by Ian Allan Printing Ltd, Hersham, Surrey, KT12 4RG

Code: 1008/B2

Distributed in the United States of America and Canada by
BookMasters Distribution services

Visit the Ian Allan Publishing website at www.ianallanpublishing.com

For John Villers,
without whom this book would not have been possible

Introduction

Besides my own efforts, the pictures in this book are mainly the work of four photographers — Brian Morrison, possibly the best known of all UK railway photographers, who has even had a main-line locomotive named after him, Roger Venning, who was very active in and around Taunton in the last days of the GWR, his friend, the late Pursey Short, who took many pictures in that part of the GWR empire immediately before and after nationalisation, sometimes on his way to National Service (ah, happy days!) with the Royal Navy at Portsmouth, Peter Treloar, born 'on the shore of Mounts Bay, where my parents owned an hotel and farm' and who, apart from his own work, has a probably unrivalled collection of GWR postcards. Other photographs have come from their collections, whilst a number of the colour pictures are the work of the late Rev Hedley Sparks,

Below: Churchward 2-6-0 No 6313 at Wolvercote Junction in 1959. *The Rev H. Sparks*

Right: Plymouth North Road in 1960 with a '94xx' a 'Hall' and brand-new Swindon-built 'Warship' taking on water. *The Rev H Sparks*

a representative of the many clergymen who have been attracted to 'God's Wonderful Railway'; I am grateful to his widow, Margaret, and his daughter, Mary, for permission to reproduce his pictures. Equally importantly, the design and sharing the selection of pictures has been the work of John Villers, one-time Cornishman and a very early member of the Great Western Society.

Over the years there have, of course, been many books published of Western Region steam, but hopefully this one will find a niche, firstly because many of the photographs have either never been seen before or else not for several decades, and secondly it will be seen as a fitting tribute in the 175th anniversary year of the Great Western Railway. The original intention had been to begin on 1 January 1948 — indeed, the book includes what I'm pretty sure is a unique picture of the very first Western Region train at Paddington

on that morning — but when Roger Venning came up with his wonderful collection of pictures taken in 1947 it seemed an awful shame not to use them, and what clinched the decision to include was the notion that it portrayed the GWR at the very end of its separate existence as it prepared to become the Western Region of British Railways.

Michael H. C. Baker
Wareham
July 2010

1947

The winter of 1946/7 was cold enough, although that of the following year would be infinitely more severe. No 7809 *Childrey Manor*, of Bath Road shed, Bristol, just released from overhaul at Swindon, stands at Taunton's Platform 7, on Saturday 8 January 1947 with the 1.20pm stopping train to Weston-super-Mare, with which it will continue to Bristol. *Roger Venning*

An immaculate Churchward Mogul, No 6368 of Westbury depot, fresh from its final GWR overhaul at Swindon, at Taunton East Yard on 11 January 1947, with the 9.05am Rogerstone–Tavistock Junction Class H coal train. Standing on the foot steps is the 'train-meeter' (Bill D'Eath), who is telling the crews which wagons need to be dropped off. Many of the wooden-bodied wagons still display the names of their private owners; the coal industry had been nationalised just 10 days earlier. *Roger Venning*

A rather less reassuring picture. Leaking prodigious amounts of steam on an icy morning in January 1947, No 6002 *King William IV* of Laira depot pulls out of Platform 7 at Taunton with the 8.30am Plymouth-Paddington express. A wheel-tapper is standing by the third carriage. In the bay No 9 is a non-corridor clerestory carriage. Built in 1927, *King William IV* would be withdrawn in September 1962. *Roger Venning*

The driver of '2721' 0-6-0PT No 2748 looks back at the approaching inspector, the latter sporting a rather grander cap than the former, as it shunts in Taunton East Yard down side attached to the obligatory shunter's truck, No 41881, on 19 March 1947. No 2748 was built in 1899 as a saddle tank, and fitted with pannier tanks in April 1923. It was withdrawn in April 1948. *Roger Venning*

'Duke' 4-4-0 No 9064 *Trevithick*, built in June 1896, is seen beside the coaling stage at its home shed — Horton Road, Gloucester — on Saturday 12 April 1947. The 'Dukes' were designed to work passenger trains over the heavily graded routes in Devon and Cornwall but in later years could be found on the Cambrian lines and elsewhere working fairly short-distance goods and passenger trains. Renumbered from 3264 in October 1946, *Trevithick* lasted until December 1949, some 18 months before the class was rendered extinct. *Roger Venning*

Taunton shed on 1 July 1947, with No 5039 *Rhuddlan Castle* of Old Oak Common (PDN) backing out towards the station to take the 4.35pm train to Paddington. *Rhuddlan Castle* was one of five 'Castles' fitted for oil burning, in December 1946; this was a short-lived experiment which cost more money than it saved, and although it made the fireman's job a lot easier it did fireboxes few favours. No 5039 reverted to coal burning in September 1948. Built in June 1935, the GWR's centenary year, it would be withdrawn exactly 29 years later. *Roger Venning*

'Bulldog' No 3443 *Chaffinch* of Taunton shed has just coupled on to Bath Road's 'Star' 4-6-0 No 4042 *Prince Albert* which has charge of the late-running 8.30am Plymouth–Paddington (10.45am ex Taunton) on 11 September 1947. The 'Bulldogs' were much used as pilots in the West Country, particularly between Exeter and Plymouth. The photographer maintains that this was his 'very favourite engine'. Built in May 1909, it was withdrawn in May 1949, just under two years before the last survivor of the class. *Roger Venning*

Above: It is sometimes forgotten that the GWR had a shed in the heart of former LNWR territory, at Gresty Lane, Crewe, and had running powers right into Manchester. The GWR's line from Wellington, Shropshire, through Market Drayton to Nantwich, and thence over LMS metals to Crewe, was a useful through route from the north, principally for goods. The relatively sparsely populated rural vastness of north Shropshire and south Cheshire through which it ran never generated much business, and in the end a single coach hauled by a pannier tank sufficed. Here, on 13 September 1947, 2-6-2T No 4103 is doing rather better with four corridors — two Churchwards, a clerestory and a modern Collett — although non-corridor carriages were equally common. By great good fortune it is passing its LMS counterpart, Stanier 2-6-4T No 2617. Stanier, of course, had spent many years at Swindon. The GWR perfected the large 2-6-2T for passenger duties, but Stanier found the 2-6-2Ts he inherited not up to much; his own version was no better, so he settled for a taper-boiler version of the excellent Fowler 2 6-4T. *Author's collection*

Above: '90xx' 4-4-0 No 9019 of Tyseley has just arrived at Taunton East Yard with a Class K branch goods from Barnstaple on Saturday 13 September 1947. The '90xx' were not exactly giants of steam, but even so the tiny (2,000gal) tender it is towing looks faintly ridiculous, as though if No 9019 went into reverse it might well trip over it. The tender is No 1128, built in 1890, with teak segments on its wheels which would make it, had it survived into the preservation era, quite valuable. The train will continue on as the 7.15pm to Durston and Bristol. One wonders how No 9019 had come to be so far from home. *Roger Venning*

GREAT WESTERN RAILWAY
MAGAZINE

SEPTEMBER · 1947   VOL. 59 · NO. 8

Pride in the Job—7
(See Page 174)

PRICE ONE PENNY

On 13 September 1947, the Saturdays-only 1.45pm Bristol–Penzance express, a continuation of the 10.40am from Wolverhampton, about to depart from Taunton behind No 5071 *Spitfire*. No 5071 was completed at Swindon in June 1938 and given the name *Clifford Castle*. To commemorate the Battle of Britain and the RAF aircraft in service at the time (and which probably saved Britain from invasion) 'Castles' Nos 5071-82 were renamed. Not all were names which history would salute, the Fairey Battle (No 5077), for example, being an aircraft which the Luftwaffe had little trouble in blasting from the skies. However, the name bestowed on No 5071 was that of the most famous aircraft of World War 2 and one which still causes a thrill when a preserved example takes to the skies. No 5071 was withdrawn in October 1963. The first carriage is one of Churchward's massive 70ft long Edwardian corridor vehicles, nicknamed 'Dreadnoughts' after the battleships then being constructed, but like them soon to be outdated. The GWR 'Dreadnoughts' had doors only at the ends and in the centre — a layout said not to be popular with the travelling public — but nevertheless had long lives. This one is still in wartime all-over brown but would receive one more overhaul (and a repaint into chocolate and cream) before withdrawal. *Roger Venning*

Norton Fitzwarren, the first station west from Taunton, on 14 September 1947. Taunton Mogul No 7314 is pulling out with the 2.30pm Taunton–Barnstaple (Victoria Road). The signal-mounted route indicator shows 'B'staple', one of four routes from here. Barnstaple was one of many destinations in Devon and Cornwall where the GWR and the Southern Railway met. Today only the SR line survives, the GWR route being long gone, although the alignment can be still traced, the bridge over the river on the approach to Barnstaple being probably the most obvious relic. The line was the last on which GWR Moguls could be seen regularly on passenger work. No 7314 was built in December 1921 and withdrawn in February 1963. *Roger Venning*

No 4037 *South Wales Borderers* heads west under the road bridge near Bradford-on-Tone, beyond Taunton, with the 10.40am Wolverhampton-Penzance express, 24 September 1947. It is hauling a mixed rake of LMS and GWR carriages. No 4037 had been built as one of Churchward's 'Stars', *Queen Philippa*, in December 1910 and was one of five which between 1925 and 1929 were rebuilt as 'Castles', being taken into Swindon Works in June 1926. There seems to have been no particular logic why these five were so treated whilst the majority of the class remained as 'Stars', although the final 10 'Stars', Nos 4063-72, were similarly rebuilt in the years 1937-40. We will meet *South Wales Borderers* later in 1958. *Roger Venning*

'Metro Tank' No 3582 stands in Taunton's bay platform on Wednesday 24 September 1947 with the 11.05am Taunton–Chard Junction branch train, composed of a Collett two-coach 'B' set. Just visible is 'Bulldog' No 3443 *Chaffinch*, the East station pilot, seen earlier piloting *Prince Albert*. Built in 1899, this 2-4-0T was, as its name implies, used on London suburban services until made redundant by the 'County' 4-4-2Ts, whereupon it migrated to the country. Fresh from overhaul at Swindon — having been probably the last of its class to receive this treatment — it was on its way home to St Blazey when commandeered by Taunton and would not reach Cornwall until July 1948. It was scrapped in November 1949. *Roger Venning*

No 5097 *Sarum Castle* accelerates under Fairwater Bridge, with the 4.50pm departure from Taunton, the 9.15am Liverpool Lime Street–Penzance, 26 September 1947. A long way from home, being a Shrewsbury engine, it is working a regular turn, having taken over from an LMS locomotive at Shrewsbury, which could have been anything from a Polmadie Pacific, filling in before returning to Scotland, to a Class 5 4-6-0, and will come off at Newton Abbot. Modern LMS Stanier-period carriages are at the head of the train, and there are likely to be GWR types further back, hidden by the smoke. No 5097 was the last prewar 'Castle', completed at Swindon in July 1939. It would be fitted with a double chimney in July 1961 but withdrawn less than two years later, in March 1963. *Roger Venning*

GREAT
WESTERN
RAILWAY

TIME TABLES

OCTOBER 6th, 1947
(and until further notice).

JAMES MILNE.   General Manager.

'Saint' No 2946 *Langford Court* of Westbury shed is about to depart from Taunton's Platform 7 on 2 October 1947 with the 11.35am stopping train to Weston-super-Mare, which will then become a Paddington express. The 'Saint' will take it as far as Bristol Temple Meads. The first two carriages are 'toplights', of the same vintage as the locomotive. *Langford Court* was completed in June 1912 and withdrawn in November 1949. *Roger Venning*

'County' 4-6-0 No 1010 gets an admiring look as it stands at the head of the 12.18pm Cardiff express in December 1947. Built in January 1946, it received the name *County of Carnarvon* — altered to *County of Caernarvon* in November 1951 — and would be withdrawn in July 1964. The train, of seven carriages, had originated as the 9.25am from Ilfracombe, which had been hauled to Taunton by Mogul No 6364; here another four carriages were added. Next to the locomotive is a clerestory Brake Third, still in wartime brown livery, whilst another corridor clerestory is standing in the bay platform, forming part of a Taunton–Bristol stopping train. The last GWR clerestories were built in 1904, and a good few survived into very early British Railways days, nearly all retaining brown livery. They had gone by the early 1950s, other than those in departmental service, and it seems unlikely that any were repainted carmine-and-cream. *Roger Venning*

THE EARLY YEARS OF NATIONALISATION

It is safe to assume that, had they been eligible to vote in the General Election of October 1951, most of my companions in Class 4A, Whitgift Middle School, Croydon, would have voted Conservative, not because we were public-school boys — in our mock election a popular prefect standing for nothing in particular easily defeated the Tory — but because we naïvely assumed that British Railways would be abolished and that the 'Big Four', in particular the Great Western Railway, would be brought back to life. We were wrong.

The separate existence of the Great Western Railway had ended at midnight on 31 December 1947, 112 years after it had begun. It was (and remains) the only British railway to reach its centenary. On the Home Service nine o'clock news on New Year's Day 1948 a recording was played of the whistles of the assembled locomotives resident at Swindon shed sounding its passing.

The nationalisation of the railways was one more step along the socialist road which had begun long before Clement Attlee's Labour Government came to power on 26 July 1945 with the huge majority of 159 seats, for the Coalition government formed on the outbreak of war in 1939 had endorsed many of the radical changes which would come about once the war was won. Seven months and five days after the nationalisation of the railways the National Health Service came into being. A year earlier the National Coal Board had taken over the mines. The fortunes of the railways and the mines had always been closely related. In 1947 a partial nationalisation of the bus and coach industry had come about but was never fully realised. The gas industry was nationalised in July 1948.

After 1948 an economic climate which showed little sign of improvement — soap, for example, was not taken off the ration until September 1950, and sweets not finally until February 1953 — and a gradual disenchantment with state-control curbed enthusiasm for nationalisation, and there was only one more such measure, affecting iron and steel (another industry closely linked to the railways), in 1950, but it was never followed through, and the incoming Conservative Government of 1951 returned practically all the firms involved to private hands.

Thus we hoped that the much-loved liveries of the Big Four would be restored. I'm not sure we thought what de-nationalisation would involve much beyond that, but, in the event, despite the formation of the Ian Allan Locospotters Club, we junior trainspotting enthusiasts were never consulted, and it would be many decades before privatisation would once again make it possible to cross the extended lawn at Paddington and board a Great Western train for Bristol and South Wales or the West of England — but not Birmingham and the North. By which time steam would be long banished except for the occasional main-line special and on various bits of the former GWR empire which the Western Region of British Railways had deemed redundant and had passed into the eager (if sometimes rather too inexperienced) hands of the enthusiast fraternity.

January 1948 certainly did not herald an immediate end to the building of GWR-designed locomotives, carriages and wagons, and for a time the old colours of Brunswick green for the locomotives and chocolate and cream for the carriages persisted, the only external difference being that 'BRITISH RAILWAYS' was applied to tenders and tank sides, and even that was done in the same style as before. Because GWR locomotives all had very stylish numberplates it was decided that they should keep these and not be renumbered; indeed, the

appearance of a Western Region train changed less than that of those of all other regions, and in black-and-white photographs one had to look closely to detect whether the photograph had been taken before or after nationalisation. After a period of experimentation British Railways decreed that all passenger express locomotives, other than the most powerful, should be painted in exactly the same shade of green which the GWR had used; larger mixed-traffic locomotives would be lined black, the rest plain black. Cream would remain for the upper works of corridor carriages, a shade of red known as carmine being applied lower down; non-corridor carriages would be dark red. Chocolate-and-cream carriages could inevitably be seen, in steadily decreasing numbers and in increasingly shabby condition, into the 1950s; indeed, wartime all-over brown had certainly not vanished, particularly on London-area suburban stock, by 1948, and most clerestories which survived into the BR era ended their days painted brown. As it turned out chocolate-and-cream never quite disappeared in the steam era, being retained on some if not all the magnificent Ocean Saloons and one or two other carriages used on special duties, and a modified version would reappear in 1956 on named trains, of which there was suddenly a great proliferation.

BR's original plan was that the elite express passenger classes — Pacifics, with the sole exception of the GWR 'Kings' — should be adorned in a shade of blue reminiscent of that used by the old Caledonian Railway. There were those GWR adherents who regretted that the 'Kings' should be so treated. I was not among them, for the shade of blue chosen, allied to black and white lining, was truly magnificent and looked splendid on all the classes which wore it. I particularly recall the impression created by No 6000 *King George V*, which in the

early days of nationalisation was based, somewhat unusually, at Bath Road, Bristol. Each year for as long as I could remember our family had made the journey from our home in Thornton Heath to my mother's sister, Aunt Agnes, who lived with Uncle Frank in a farm cottage close to the Shrewsbury-Crewe line midway between the first and second stations, Hadnall and Yorton, out of Shrewsbury. We regularly took the train to Shrewsbury for a visit, amongst other things, to the Granada cinema on Castle Hill, a hundred yards or so from the station, and by 1948, when I was 11, I was allowed to make my own way there and spent many happy hours on Shrewsbury station. (I still do!) Practically every type of LMS-designed locomotive could be seen, as well as the seemingly indestructible ex-LNWR 0-8-0s, plus that company's few surviving (and rather more fragile) passenger locomotives — 2-4-2Ts and 0-6-2Ts — and some ancient 0-6-0 goods types which were entrusted with branch-line passenger work. The last of the big, handsome but short-lived 4-4-0s and 4-6-0s, of which the 'Prince of Wales' was the best known in the Shrewsbury area, were now all gone. There were few GWR designs which did not appear at Shrewsbury, but this paragraph began with *King George V*, and we will return to that noble class of locomotives of which No 6000 was the precursor (no pun intended).

Almost invariably our Paddington-Birkenhead express would be hauled by a 'King' as far as Wolverhampton, where any type of passenger locomotive might take over; the preferred choice was a 'Castle' or 'Star', but it could well be a 'Hall', a 'Grange', a 'Manor' or a Churchward Mogul. 'Kings' did not normally appear at Shrewsbury. However, as noted, the one exception was *King George V* itself, for a regular duty for this locomotive while based at Bristol took it over the North & West main line between the West Country and Shrewsbury — which was how I came to see it, resplendent in blue, reversing on the Abbey Foregate triangle at the south end of the station, having arrived with a train bound for Liverpool Lime Street and prior to relieving a 'Coronation' Pacific on a southbound express. Honesty compels me to add that, whilst I thought the 'Kings' incomparable, the sight of blue-liveried No 46220 *Coronation*, newly overhauled at Crewe Works and pulling out over the ferociously sharp curve at the

Above: Uncle Frank and Aunt Agnes.

Left: Spangles were introduced in 1948.

Below: Petrol was still rationed in 1948.

The final examples of the first generation of London trams were taken out of service in 1952.

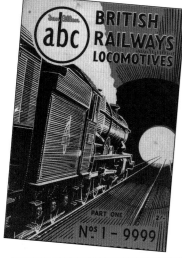

north end of the station, was simply breathtaking. That curve had been the undoing of a North-West express on 15 October 1907, when, due into Shrewsbury at 2.05am, hauled by 'Experiment' 4-6-0 No 2052 *Stephenson*, it failed to slow to the stipulated 10mph and instead hurtled past the Crewe Bank signalbox at around 60mph. Twenty people, including the driver and fireman, died in the resulting pile-up, several of the wooden-bodied carriages — Dean clerestories and low-roofed LNWR types — telescoping. The reason for the disaster was never discovered. As may be imagined, it caused a tremendous sensation in the area, and Uncle Frank, then a schoolboy, recalled the horrific thrill of being taken to see the wreckage the next morning.

The GWR handed over to British Railways a grand total of 3,857 locomotives, all but one of them steam, the exception being diesel-electric shunter No 2, the forerunner of those that are still with us today. With these came 37 diesel railcars — far and away the most successful examples of such vehicles which had been introduced by the main-line companies and which also led to the subsequent widespread introduction of the diesel multiple-unit, as it came to be known.

Top of the range were the 30 'Kings', whilst the mainstay of main-line long distance passenger services were the 141 'Castles'. The 47 'Stars', although dating back to Edwardian times, still had a significant role to play; indeed, one shedmaster in the early 1950s, when asked which was his preferred 'Castle',

replied: "A late-series 'Star'." Churchward's two-cylinder 'Saints', of which there were also 47 still at work, were by now largely confined to secondary duties, although peak times could see them once more on express duties, and those based at Hereford were much appreciated locally, being dubbed 'Hereford Castles'. Most modern of all the larger passenger locomotives were the 30 postwar 'Counties', developments of the 'Modified Halls' ('6959' series), of which there were 22. There were no fewer than 258 of the original 'Halls' — locomotives of inestimable value, which could be seen hauling just about anything from named expresses to lengthy coal trains. Close relations were the 80 'Granges' and the 20 'Manors', the smallest of all the GWR 4-6-0s.

It had been intended that the 'Granges' and 'Manor's would completely replace the Churchward 2-6-0s, containing as they did parts of these estimable mixed-traffic locomotives, but the outbreak of war frustrated this intention, much to the delight of all who held in the Moguls in great esteem. Thus there were 241 of these, including 20 of the later Collett variety. Well on the way to extinction were the 12 remaining 'Aberdare' 2-6-0s, goods locomotives gradually being made redundant by Churchward, Collett and Riddles 2-8-0s.

The Collett mixed-traffic 4-6-0s had much reduced the once numerous 4-4-0s, those remaining comprising 45 'Bulldogs', 11 'Dukes' (the most antique-looking of all GWR locomotives, with their curved, outside frames, huge domes and minimal cabs and, in some cases, towing tenders which appeared to have scarcely sufficient coal capacity to keep the average waiting-room fire supplied for more than a few weeks) and 29 '9000s' (looking scarcely any more modern), some of which had briefly carried the names of belted Earls.

The heaviest freight duties were the responsibility of 167 standard Churchward and Collett 2-8-0s, 45 Robinson-designed ROD 2-8-0s and the nine '47xx' mixed-traffic 2 8-0s. All the GWR-designed 2-4-0s were long gone, but three little engines of this wheel arrangement, inherited from the Midland & South West Junction Railway, had found favour with Swindon and remained at work. The 'Dean Goods' 0-6-0s, of which there were 54, refused to die, and there were also 11 0-6-0s which had belonged to the Cambrian Railways and which, fitted with 'Dean Goods' boilers, were considered their equal and could still be found on both passenger and goods duties amongst the Welsh hills and mountains. There were 118 Collett '2251' 0-6-0s.

This brings us to the tank engine, a design the GWR took to its ample bosom and clasped tightly — none more so than the 0-6-0 pannier tank. Wherever one ventured on the GWR (other than on the Cambrian section), one was always likely to stumble across several examples of Collett's '57xx', there being no fewer than 762 of these, including 11 fitted with condensers for working over the Metropolitan Underground lines to Smithfield meat market. The Cambrian, along with other sections with weight restrictions, had their own lightweight versions, and then there were the larger-wheeled examples which were mainly intended for passenger work, specifically (although not exclusively) push-pull. These included the 25 '54xx', the 40 '64xx', the 60 '67xx' and the 30 '74xx'. Pre-dating all these were late-19th — and early-20th-century conversions from saddle tanks — four '1501s', 36 '1854s', 21 '655s', one '1813', 44 '1901s' and 110 '2021s'. Two of the '1854s' and one '2021' remained in their original saddle-tank state. At the other extreme were 10 postwar, taper-boiler '94xx'. Finally there were the five outside-cylinder, short-wheelbase '1361' 0 6-0 saddle tanks and their six '1366' pannier-tank successors. An unbiased observer might well wonder why such a variety was necessary, but the GWR would no doubt have considered this a question beneath its dignity to answer.

The GWR had inherited an awful lot of tank engines from the companies which worked up and down the Welsh valleys. Some of these it had 'Westernised' with new boilers and fittings. The 0-6-0s numbered 26 but did not include two Stroudley 'Terriers' acquired by the Weston, Clevedon & Portishead, nor the two narrow-gauge Welshpool & Llanfair locomotives.

What the Welsh railways loved above all else was the 0-6-2T, and there were 191 still at work, many rebuilt by the GWR. There were also 200 of the GWR's own '56xx' and '66xx' classes, built in the 1920s very much with the Welsh Valley traffic in mind. A solitary 0-8-2T was No 1358, inherited from the Port Talbot Railway.

The 0-4-2T might reasonably have been considered an outdated wheel arrangement by the time of the Grouping in 1923, but the GWR paid little heed to fashion, building 75 '14xx' for push-pull work and, somewhat inexplicably, 20 of the otherwise identical '58xx', which were not push-pull-fitted and must surely have been difficult to keep fully employed. In addition there remained three of the Dean 0-4-2Ts and two narrow gauge examples inherited from the Corris Railway.

The 2-4-0T had been popular on the GWR in earlier days, and 10 Dean examples, once extensively employed on London suburban work, were still around, there were two from the Cambrian and one from the Looe & Liskeard Railway.

The 0-4-0T was represented by 17 shunters, 11 of them absorbed from Welsh companies, the other six being GWR-designed locomotives of the '11xx' class.

This brings us to the 2-6-2T, a wheel arrangement almost as popular with the GWR as the 0-6-0PT. To begin at the beginning, the least amongst them, size-wise, — albeit highly regarded — were the 11 '44xx'. Next were the slightly larger '45xx' and '55xx', of which there were 175. Then come the big boys, quivalents of the various LMS and LNER 2-6-4Ts: most numerous were the 149 '51xx' in the '41xx' and '51xx' series, their derivatives the five '31xx', the 10 '81xx' and the 70 higher-pressure '61xx' built especially for work in the London area. There were a couple of Welsh ex-Alexandra Docks 2-6-2Ts and — something none of the other 'Big Four' companies could claim in 1947 — three mountaineering narrow-gauge 2-6-2Ts, representing the entire locomotive stock of the Vale of Rheidol line.

Finally there were the big goods tank engines, something else in which the GWR specialised and proved better at than anyone else. There were 151 '42xx' and '5205' 2-8-0Ts and 54 '72xx' versions rebuilt with a pair of trailing wheels and extended bunkers, giving them a range that almost matched that of a 2-8-0 tender engine.

1948

The first BR train to leave Paddington, the 12.05am sleeper to Birkenhead on 1 January 1948, headed by No 5032 *Usk Castle*, allocated to Stafford Road, Wolverhampton. Built in May 1934, the locomotive would be fitted with a double chimney in May 1959 and withdrawn in September 1962. Dawn would be breaking as the train left Chester, where a '51xx' 2-6-2T would probably take charge, and arrival at Birkenhead Woodside would be at 8.06am, although the final destination in the timetable was given as 'Liverpool Landing Stage', which would be reached by ferry at 8.28am (see inset). *Author's collection*

A picture which perfectly illustrates the joint nature of Shrewsbury station. On 6 March 1948 No 28370, an ancient LNWR Webb 'Cauliflower' 0-6-0, its design dating to 1887, gets a once-over from its driver whilst the fireman looks back from the top of the tender at the guard who is approaching, no doubt with news of the weight of the three GWR corridor carriages it is about to haul, all stations to Hereford. Its shedplate, 4A, is that of Bletchley, so it is a long way from home unless it has just been transferred to Shrewsbury. On the opposite platform is a Collett corridor carriage, forming part of a Paddington express. The lower-quadrant signal, mounted low down to clear the overall roof, is down, which means the express has the road; the stopper will follow it out but swing sharply in the opposite direction over the River Severn. *C. C. B. Herbert*

However grand were the 'Kings', 'Castles' and 'Stars', the most ubiquitous of all Swindon designs was the pannier tank, far and away the most numerous being the '57xx' class. Still in GWR green, No 3675, of Laira depot, is seen west of Creech St Michael at 4.25pm on 27 March 1948 with the Highbridge–Tiverton Junction Class J pick-up goods. Looking out of the cab is fireman Bob Chudleigh, of Taunton shed. No 3675 was built in June 1940 (production continuing throughout the war) and withdrawn in December 1965. *Pursey Short*

Hauled by No 5019 *Treago Castle* of Bristol Bath Road depot, the Sundays-only 9.30am Plymouth–Paddington express passes Victory Crossing signalbox, west of Norton Fitzwarren, at 12.15pm on 28 March 1948. Although still with its number on the buffer-beam, GWR-style, *Treago Castle* has the legend 'BRITISH RAILWAYS' on its tender. The first three carriages are all ex LMS, still in that company's dark-red livery, but, as will become apparent, the Western Region made pretty free with LMS-design carriages, at least one of which could often be seen in a train otherwise composed of GWR-design vehicles. Behind the signalbox is a very substantial-looking telegraph pole, a common sight in those days. No 5019 was built in July 1932 and withdrawn in September 1962. *Pursey Short*

The photographer took this picture on 4 April 1948 as his train was leaving Bristol Temple Meads for Portsmouth, where he was based during National Service in the Royal Navy. One of the venerable but seemingly indestructible 'Dean Goods' 0-6-0s, No 2578 of St Philip's Marsh depot (SPM), has got itself sandwiched between a pair of 'Toad' brake vans whilst shunting a permanent-way train.

No 2578 was one of the final three members of its class, completed at Swindon in January 1899, two years before the death of Queen Victoria, and lasted long enough to witness the coronation of her great, great grand-daughter, Queen Elizabeth II, not being withdrawn until September 1953. *Pursey Short*

'County' No 1007 *County of Brecknock* of Bath Road depot arriving at Bristol Temple Meads at 5.30pm on Sunday 4 April 1948 with an express from Paddington. Completed at Swindon in December 1945, No 1007 and its 29 companions were the ultimate development of the two-cylinder 4-6-0 which had begun with the 'Saints'. As can be seen they looked every inch a Swindon design, but variations on the theme were their 'Modified Hall'-type plate frames, a new Standard No 15 boiler with a pressure of 280lb, 6ft 3in coupled wheels, flat sided tender, and continuous splashers surmounted with a straight nameplate. Some of the publicity at the time of their introduction declared them to be 'Improved Castles', which did them no favours. Apart from five at Stafford Road, Wolverhampton, at the time of the photograph the entire class was concentrated either at Old Oak Common or in the West Country. *Pursey Short*

One of the early results of nationalisation was a series of trials involving locomotives of the 'Big Four'. Stanier-designed LMS Pacific No 46236 *City of Bradford*, shown here at Westbury at 12 noon on 19 May 1948, worked on the West of England main line. Built as a streamliner in July 1939, it scarcely had time to show its potential before the outbreak of World War 2, during which it was called upon to perform prodigious feats of haulage. Unlike the rival LNER 'A4s' all the Stanier Pacifics lost their streamlining during or soon after the war, and No 46236 is seen here, defrocked, gleaming in lined black and attached to the clerestory roofed dynamometer car, which seems to be getting as much attention from the assembled spectators as the locomotive. The train is the 8.30am Plymouth-Paddington, from which the photographer had just alighted on his way to Portsmouth. The trials were fairly inconclusive, later analysis suggesting that if a development of the 'King', in which design Stanier had been intimately involved, had been contemplated, a 4-8-0 rather than a Pacific would have been the ideal for the West of England main line, in view of the fearsome gradients west of Newton Abbot. *Pursey Short*

Although the GWR took great pride in its claim that the 'Cheltenham Flyer' was for a time in the late 1920s and early '30s the fastest train in the world, it had to admit defeat in 1935, when Sir Nigel Gresley introduced his remarkable 'A4' streamlined Pacifics on the LNER and quickly established with the 'Silver Jubilee', 'Coronation' and 'West Riding Limited' speed records beyond the reach of the GWR — or any other British railway. Eventually, in 1938, one of the 'A4s', *Mallard*, was worked up to 126mph, which remains the fastest speed ever recorded by a steam locomotive. Not surprisingly *Mallard* was chosen to represent the LNER in the Locomotive Exchanges of 1948, being seen at North Road, Plymouth, in May of that year. Unfortunately *Mallard* suffered a failure later in the week and was replaced by another 'A4', No 60033 *Seagull*. *Author's collection*

The up 'Cornish Riviera' in all its chocolate-and-cream glory at Bishopsteignton at 1.20pm on Tuesday 21 September 1948. Headed by newly overhauled No 6001 *King Edward VII* of Old Oak Common, which seems to be making light of its 13-coach train, the locomotive is in British Railways lined blue, complete with smokebox numberplate. Completed at Swindon, along with Nos 6002-5, in July 1927, it would be was withdrawn in September 1962, having completed almost two million miles in a 35-year career spent on top-link duties. *Pursey Short*

The down 'Cornish Riviera', photographed at one of the best-known locations on the entire system — Shaldon Bridge, alongside the Teign Estuary just beyond Teignmouth — at 2.10pm on 21 September 1948. The locomotive is No 6025 *King Henry III*, of Old Oak Common, while the seemingly minuscule vehicle at the head of the train is a bullion van carrying valuables to be loaded on to a transatlantic liner, possibly belonging to the French Line, at Plymouth. The rest of the train is made up of no fewer than 13 carriages of uniform vintage, being of very modern late-prewar/early wartime design. The seventh vehicle is a 70ft dining car. Although the carriages are still in chocolate- and-cream livery the locomotive has been repainted in the attractive but short lived blue with red, cream and grey lining, as applied to British Railways' most powerful passenger locomotives. *Pursey Short*

Inset: One of the most popular PSVs of the immediate postwar era was the Bedford/Duple OB. A preserved example with a Devon registration is seen on its way to Teignmouth. *Author*

1949

At around 3.30 pm on 19 February 1949, Collett 2-8-0 No 2895 from faraway Birkenhead — the most northerly ex-GWR depot — has the road with a down goods train at Meads Crossing, near Somerset Bridge, Bridgwater. Still in GWR livery, it had been built in November 1938 and would be withdrawn in April 1965. Birkenhead, from 1923 a joint LMS/GWR facility, would retain steam longer than almost any other WR depot, although in its final years it was firmly in the hands of the London Midland Region and saw only ex-LMS and BR Standard locomotives. *Pursey Short*

In experimental apple-green livery and with tender lettered 'BRITISH RAILWAYS', No 7011 *Banbury Castle* heads a 12-coach Wolverhampton–Penzance express at Huntworth, near Bridgwater, on 19 February 1949. The first two carriages are of the GWR design, the next six LMS, with more GWR vehicles bringing up the rear. A Bristol Bath Road locomotive, No 7011 was one of the second batch of postwar 'Castles', being just eight months old at the time of the photograph. *Pursey Short*

With the leaves bursting out on the trees above the station, No 1014 *County of Glamorgan* speeds through Durston station on a fine spring morning, 14 April 1949, with an express from Paddington to Bristol and Taunton. Completed in February 1946, *County of Glamorgan* received its nameplates in March 1948. Here still in GWR livery, it would be withdrawn in April 1964. In the station stands 0-6-0PT No 4689 of Yeovil shed, with a goods train for the Taunton branch. *Pursey Short*

0-6-0PT No 1863 shunting at Dudley on 26 April 1949. This locomotive was built as a Dean saddle tank in 1890 and later converted to a pannier tank, a type beloved of the GWR and to be found in its many varieties everywhere on the system, working just about every sort of duty from its favourite one of shunting through to occasional haulage of named expresses in the remoter parts of Wales. No 1863's open cab ensured the crew were supplied with whatever fresh air was to be had in this smoky part of the Black Country. The extensive network of lines at Dudley, once owned jointly by the GWR and the LNWR, have quite vanished, part of the site being occupied by the Black Country Museum, where, even if there is no railway presence, one can savour the delights of travel by canal barge, tram, bus and trolleybus (see inset). *Author's collection*

On 11 June 1949 No 7815 *Fritwell Manor*, of Gloucester shed, pulls out under the impressive gantry at Southampton Central with the 4.30pm Southampton Terminus-Cheltenham Town. Four carriages, the first a 'toplight', probably represents a generous allocation for this service, which traversed the Midland & South Western Junction Railway by way of Andover, Swindon Town and Cricklade, joining the Kingham-Cheltenham line at Andoversford Junction. 'Manors' and Churchward Moguls were the usual motive power, although Southern Maunsell 2-6-0s also regularly worked the route. *Fritwell*

Manor was built in January 1939 and withdrawn in November 1965, while the great gantry lasted until the end of the 1980s. The Army, on the edge of Salisbury Plain, was a good customer for the MSWJ, but the line has long been closed, although a section just north of Swindon has been revived and now sees steam trains. It hopes to reach Cricklade, and in its workshop a group including some former Swindon Works craftsmen are restoring a 'toplight' carriage very like that in the picture. *Pursey Short*

No 231, a former Barry Railway 'B'-class 0-6-2T, at Barry shed on 19 June 1949. A Sharp Stewart locomotive dating from February 1890, it looks in a rather sad state, with dome cover removed and placed on the firebox, and may well have carried out its last duties. The class, originally 25 strong, was used exclusively on coal traffic, and the locomotives were not fitted with vacuum brakes. One was scrapped as early as October 1922, and many of the others were rebuilt with GWR boilers and bunkers, which radically altered their appearance. All but two of those in original condition were withdrawn during the drastic decline in coal traffic in the early 1930s, but No 231 outlived all the modernised locomotives and was the last of its class when taken out of service in October 1949. *Author's collection*

Received wisdom regarding the '47xx' 2-8-0s suggests that they saw widespread use on express passenger work only at the end of their careers, in the late 1950s and early '60s. Whilst this may have been largely true this picture provides evidence that they could certainly be found on such duties rather earlier. No 4703 of Laira (LA) depot is passing Powderham, near Starcross, at six o'clock on the evening of 16 July 1949 with the 1.30pm Paddington to Paignton express. It was only a few minutes late and presumably the 2-8-0 had been in charge throughout which was pretty good going for an eight-coupled locomotive with 5ft 8in driving wheels with this 12-coach restaurant-car express. Built in 1922, No 4703 was one of the final three members of the class to be withdrawn, in May 1964. *Pursey Short*

The well-known setting of Weymouth Quay, on 22 July 1949. No 1367, one of the six outside-cylinder pannier tanks of the '1366' class, dating from 1934, hauls the afternoon Paddington-bound Channel Islands boat train under the road bridge (which to this day often floods) beside the lifting bridge which allows boats in and out of the inner harbour. There is no sign of the bell mounted on the locomotive nor the man who walked in front, certainly in later years, to keep the tracks clear and warn motorists not to park too close, a growing hazard as motor traffic increased. Two distinctly elderly saloons are parked on the left. No 1367 will haul the train as far as the sidings beside Weymouth Town station where it will hand over to a 'Castle'. Eventually the former GWR route was downgraded to branch line and singled, boat trains being transferred to the Southern Region. No 1367 was withdrawn in October 1967. *Pursey Short*

Inset: In July 1979 the scene was recreated when the Great Western Society's Vintage Train visited Weymouth Quay, albeit not hauled by a '1366'. *Author*

The most sensational event on the Western Region in 1949 was the arrival of a gas-turbine locomotive. Dubbed 'the jet engine' by the popular press, it was like nothing seen before. Ordered from the Swiss firm of Brown-Boveri in 1940 but delayed by the war, No 18000 is seen here with the Western Region trial train, which, rather curiously, consists of three elderly Edwardian 'toplight' corridor carriages, a three coach 1920s restaurant-car set and the dynamometer car. No 18000 was a 115-ton A1A-A1A locomotive, its gas-turbine 'turboshaft' generator being started up by a diesel engine, the latter normally being used when running light between Old Oak Common depot and Paddington station. *Author's collection*

British Railways inherited many thousands of horses, and although their numbers were dwindling rapidly they survived into the 1950s. A placid-looking pair of former GWR greys pose along with their carter at Paddington goods depot c1949. The story goes that in Basingstoke — a town served hitherto by both the Southern and Great Western and where the latter's Thornycroft lorries were built — shortly after nationalisation a lady with inflated ideas of her own importance rebuked a carter for letting his horse stand partly on the pavement whilst making a delivery. 'You know you are all servants of the public now, my good man'. 'In that case,' he replied, plucking a hair from the horse's tail and handing it to her, 'this is your share, madam.' The last railway horse on street work was retired in 1959. 'Horses at Work', part of the Bradford Industrial Museum, tells of the history of the railway horse and keeps alive and working some of the breeds used. *Author's collection*

'Saint' 4-6-0 No 2950 *Taplow Court* of Bath Road shed, Bristol, passing Powderham at 5.20 on the afternoon of 23 July 1949 with a Paignton-Manchester London Road express. The 11 carriages, all of them from the Collett era, would nearly all appear to still be in GWR livery, but the 37-year-old 'Saint' has a BR smokebox numberplate. It also carries the train-reporting number (593) on a small, LMS-style board, rather than the usual large GWR-type number. The 25 'Courts' were the final 'Saints', appearing between October 1911 and April 1913. *Taplow Court* lasted until April 1952, and was clearly still thought capable of performing top link duties right to the end. The elderly 8hp saloon on the right looks rather like an early 1930s Austin. *Pursey Short*

Milk from the West Country was once big business for the railways, and the haulage of the heavy up train from Penzance to Paddington was one for which the '47xx' 2-8-0s were ideally suited. No 4700, of Old Oak Common depot, has charge of the 12 tankers plus the passenger brake van as it overtakes a Citroën and a Vauxhall, being seen passing Powderham at 6.20pm (*Dick Barton, Special Agent*, along with faithful accomplices Jock and Snowy, will be starting on the Home Service in 25 minutes) on 23 July 1949. *Pursey Short*

A picture which demonstrates just how 'joint' the lines through High Wycombe and Princes Risborough were. The London extension of the Great Central Railway was opened in 1899 and in 1906 the Great Western & Great Central Joint line from Northolt Junction to Ashendon was completed, giving the former railway a shorter route from Paddington to Birmingham and the North, allowing it to compete more effectively with the LNWR, and the latter a route into Marylebone which did not rely on Metropolitan Railway co-operation. Swindon-built 2-6-2T No 6166 has charge of the 11.20am Marylebon-Princes Risborough on 17 December 1949. The carriages are ex-LNER stock, the second having been built by the Great Central Railway. *C. R. L. Coles*

1950

Taunton station at 10.45am on Saturday 8 April 1950. No 6009 *King Charles II*, of Old Oak Common, is pulling out with the 8.30am Plymouth–Paddington express. It is painted in the short-lived lined blue livery, which was worn only by the 'Kings' (and which suited them rather well), the 'Merchant Navies', the 'Princess Royal' and 'Coronation' Pacifics and most of the LNER-design Pacifics. The leading carriage, a Churchward 'toplight', is in carmine and cream. The combination was a most pleasing one but the blue was said not to weather well and the 'Kings' on their next overhaul reverted to their traditional green. *King Charles II* was withdrawn in September 1962. *Pursey Short* k

Tyseley shed on 20 April 1950. Princess Margaret — the royal personage, not the 'Star'-class locomotive — is visiting Stratford-upon-Avon, and the three locomotives prepared for royal duty are lined up. In the foreground is No 4980 *Wrottesley Hall*, to its left is No 7001 *Sir James Milne*, whilst bringing up the rear is No 5000 *Launceston Castle*. By now GWR lined green has been decided upon for express passenger locomotives so the 'Castles' are little changed in appearance from GWR days other than smokebox numberplates, a modification of their black and orange lining and the 'lion on a unicycle' on their tenders. 'Halls', being mixed-traffic locomotives, wear LNWR-style lined black. *Launceston Castle* will be withdrawn in October 1964, *Sir James Milne*, despite being fitted with a double chimney, a year earlier in September 1963, and *Wrottesley Hall* in July 1963. *Author's collection*

Wellington, Somerset, at 12.40pm on Sunday 24 April 1950. GWR livery has not yet vanished, and Churchward Mogul No 5355 of Pontypool Road depot, at the head of a fully fitted freight, is galloping along the through line taking a run at the famous bank which the driver is intending to surmount without assistance. Built in August 1918, No 5355 was withdrawn in April 1959. *Pursey Short*

A rather sad scene at Machynlleth, on the Corris Railway, on 30 April 1950. This narrow-gauge line had been opened in the 1850s and had prospered, carrying both slate and passengers. Decline set in during the early part of the 20th century, buses took the passenger traffic away, and acquisition by the GWR in 1930 did little to improve its situation. British Railways closed it completely at the beginning of 1948, but the two locomotives eventually found a home elsewhere in Wales, as did some of the slate wagons seen here. A standard-gauge siding is just visible on the far left. Eventually after much negotiation and hard work a section of the Corris Railway reopened and began carrying passengers in 2002. *Author's collection*

Rivals pool their resources on Mortehoe Bank as Southern 'M7' 0-4-4TNo 30036 gives the six carriages of the Swindon-built '4575' 2-6-2T No 5501 of Taunton shed a helping shove on the very last leg of their journey from Paddington at 5.14pm on Saturday 1 July 1950. The first four carriages are of GWR origin, some probably still in chocolate-and-cream livery, whilst the other two, ex-LMS, are still in that company's deep red. The train is approaching Mortehoe & Woolacombe station, whence it is a gentle run down to Ilfracombe with wonderful views, on a clear day, across the Bristol Channel to South Wales and the Gower Peninsula. At that time paddle-steamers were still much in demand, conveying holidaymakers along the Devon and Somerset coast and across to South Wales, and liners still sailed out of Avonmouth on their way to the West Indies. The line between Ilfracombe and Barnstaple was Southern territory, Western Region trains reaching Barnstaple from Taunton by way of Norton Fitzwarren and Dulverton. Southern trains coming out of Exeter left the Western's West of England main line at Cowley Bridge Junction, Coleford Junction and Portsmouth Arms. This still exists, although the line beyond Barnstaple has gone. *Pursey Short*

Worcester shed's No 6851 *Hurst Grange* on the turntable at Weymouth, with a deceptively rural backdrop, on 27 August 1950. The locomotive is painted in unlined black, but a touch of colour is provided by the pale-blue background to its' name — and numberplates. Built at Swindon in November 1937 using parts from a Churchward Mogul, it would be withdrawn in August 1965. No 'Granges' survived to be preserved, but one is being reconstructed at Llangollen. *Pursey Short*

One of the most remarkable survivals into British Railways days involved a group of four-wheel carriages built by the GWR in the 1890s. Even then they were considered distinctly old-fashioned, being confined to certain branch lines and London suburban services, but they were very useful in that they could accommodate a lot of people in not very much space, if not in much comfort, and were still working out of Paddington in the early 1920s. The survivors were dispersed deep into the country and could be found, for instance, on the Burry Port & Gwendraeth Valley line, which had severe restrictions and saw no bogie stock until 1939. Although some specially built, low-roof bogie carriages then appeared there, this was not the end of the four-wheelers, and some could still be found until the branch closed in 1953. They were retained for miners' services, and a rake of four is seen here, hauled by pannier tank No 9634 of Duffryn Yard, with the miners embarking by way of the footsteps, having trudged along the track at the termination of their shift. *Author's collection*

1951

Paddington station on Easter Sunday — 24 March 1951 — 'Castle' No 4096 *Highclere Castle* has just arrived with empty stock to form an express for Bristol whilst No 6005 *King George II* is arriving, on time, at Platform 10 with the 07.30am from Shrewsbury. Note the row of taxis, most of them of prewar origin.

It was quite common for main-line locomotives to bring in empty stock whilst awaiting their next long distance turn. *Highclere Castle* was built in June 1926 and withdrawn in January 1963, *King George II* was built in July 1927 and withdrawn in November 1962. *Brian Morrison*

At 5pm on 24 March 1951 the up 'North Mail' from Penzance to Manchester London Road and Liverpool Lime Street steams past Cockwood beside the River Exe in the charge of No 1024 *County of Pembroke*, of Stafford Road, Wolverhampton. The TPO looks to be No 796, a 50ft-long vehicle completed at Swindon in October 1933, originally liveried in chocolate and cream but by now repainted in Post Office red. *Pursey Short*

An immaculate 'Modified Hall', No 6966 *Witchingham Hall* of Westbury shed, ex works, leaving Starcross on 24 March 1951 with a four-coach down stopping train consisting of three Colletts and a 70ft-long 'toplight'. A 'Hall' in lined-out black BR livery could look distinctly stylish. To the left of the train is the tall tower of the pumping station for Brunel's atmospheric railway. From Starcross one could (and still can) take a passenger foot ferry to the other side of the Exe Estuary and the former LSWR Exmouth branch. Apart from the disappearance of the signalbox the scene is little changed today, steam still putting in an appearance from time to time, notably on the regular 'Torbay Expresses'. *Pursey Short*

No 7805 *Broome Manor*, of Banbury depot, is about to enter Whiteball Tunnel, near Wellington, Somerset, with a down goods, just before noon on Sunday 22 April 1951. Some three years and four months after the creation of British Railways the locomotive still sports GWR initials on its tender. The platelayers' hut, reached by a neat flight of steps, is of interest looking like a possibly cut-down four-wheel carriage body. *Broome Manor* was completed at Swindon in March 1938 and withdrawn in December 1964. *Pursey Short*

Two locomotives working flat-out as they heave a heavy goods train up Wellington Bank at noon on Sunday, 22 April 1951. The banker, still wearing GWR livery, is 2-6-2T No 4136, completed in the first months of World War 2, in December 1939, while the train engine is Collett 2-8-0 No 3845, also built during the war, in April 1942. Standing by the telegraph pole, more or less level with the 'Toad' brake van, is the photographer's father. No 4136 was a Taunton locomotive, but the 2-8-0 was based at Reading. Both locomotives were withdrawn in June 1964. The 2-6-2T was broken up at Cashmore's yard, but the 2 8-0 had the good luck to be sent to Dai Woodham's yard at Barry. This meant it was left to languish, more or less intact, for many years and was eventually bought for preservation. It has since had a number of homes but has not yet been restored to working order. *Pursey Short*

No 1925 on the Swindon dump, 10 June 1951. The initials 'GWR' are still visible (someone has been cleaning them so they show through), and although the numberplate has gone the initials of the saddle tank's last home, Southall, can be seen behind the front buffer-beam. The '1901' class, of which No 1925 was an example, was introduced in 1881. All were built as saddle tanks, but most were converted to panniers in later life. However, this never happened to No 1925 which was one of the very few to survive in its original condition into BR days. *Author's collection*

A less-than-pristine 'King', No 6007 *King William III*, heads through Ruscombe, near Twyford, on 5 July 1951, returning a train of empty milk tankers to the West of England for a refill. An Old Oak Common locomotive, one of 13 'Kings' based there at this time, it would be withdrawn in September 1962. Milk traffic outlived the steam era on British Rail, although it was in decline by the early 1960s and finally ended in 1980, when trains from South Wales and the West of England to London ceased running. *Brian Morrison*

Get 'em young! A family in Sydney Gardens, Bath, watches No 7019 *Fowey Castle* pass by at the head of a Paddington-Weston-super-Mare express. Based at Bath Road, Bristol, the locomotive was completed at Swindon by British Railways in May 1949. The time is 3.10pm, the date 4 September 1951, and summer is clearly still with us. Even in those days it was a little surprising that the public could sit and stand in such close proximity to speeding trains; that they can still do so nearly 60 years later is nothing short of astonishing. *Pursey Short*

Another Sydney Gardens scene on 4 September 1951, this time featuring 'Dean Goods' No 2340, of St Philip's Marsh, Bristol, with a Westbury-bound pick-up goods. By this date such workings probably operated at a loss and would continue to do so, a millstone around the railways' neck, until they finally disappeared not long after steam had gone. These elderly 0-6-0s, originating in 1883, were quite possibly the best investment the GWR ever made. Equally at home on goods or local passenger work, they originally numbered 260 locomotives. Around 40 were still at work at this time; the last, No 2516, was not withdrawn until 1957 and is today one of the star exhibits at STEAM — Museum of the Great Western Railway in Swindon. *Pursey Short*

Despite being small in number (15) the Cambrian Railways 'Large Belpaire Goods' 0-6-0s fitted into the GWR pattern of things — all, that is, except for three which were sent to Swindon in 1922 and never emerged, being broken up there and then. One other was destroyed in an accident in 1933, but the rest, fitted with Swindon boilers, went about their Mid-Wales duties into the 1950s. No 895 is seen 'abroad' at Worcester on 9 September 1951. Worcester is not all that far from Wales, and the shiny smokebox suggests that it might have just come out of the works there. No 895 was one of the final three, being withdrawn in October 1954. The author came across No 895 in August of that year, at Whitchurch, watching her arrive from Oswestry with a train of three GWR-design carriages (one an almost-new Hawksworth 'bow-ender'), then, after some gentle shunting, take itself off to the small shed, in which it was tucked up for the night, ready to return to Wales early next morning. *Author's collection*

The first BR Standard locomotives to enter service were the 'Britannia' Pacifics, No 70000 *Britannia* emerging from Crewe Works in January 1951, and during the course of that year eight were allocated to the Western Region. That their arrival was greeted with less than unalloyed joy probably says more about entrenched GWR attitudes than the quality of these handsome locomotives, which proved themselves to be excellent machines elsewhere, particularly on the Great Eastern main lines. Here, on 6 November 1951, No 70020 *Mercury*, of Old Oak Common, stands at Paddington's Platform 4 with the 6.55pm to Swansea. The first carriage is a rebuilt 70ft-long 'toplight' restaurant car, the rest the usual collection of mixed vintage GWR vehicles, ranging from the 'toplight' pre-1914 to the Hawksworth post-1945 era. The first BR standard carriages appeared in 1950, and one or two rakes of these, with GWR restaurant cars, appeared on named trains, including one short-lived through Paddington-Stratford-upon-Avon train marking the Festival of Britain, but it would be a while before they replaced Hawksworth carriages on the 'Cornish Riviera'. The Western Region 'Britannias' eventually migrated to Cardiff Canton, where they put in some good work. *Brian Morrison*

1952

King George VI died at Sandringham in February 1952. His funeral train — the former LNER Royal Train, comprising a mixture of GNR-, NER- and LNER-built carriages — is seen here on 15 February passing Iver on its way to Windsor behind No 4082 *Windsor Castle*. One glance at the front end would have told any knowledgeable enthusiast that this was not the original No 4082, which at the time was undergoing overhaul at Swindon and could not be made ready in time; instead one of the postwar 'Castles', No 7013 *Bristol Castle*, was substituted, the two locomotives swapping identities permanently. The locomotive displays the Royal Crest on both sides and carries four headlamps, the uppermost surmounted by a crown. *Brian Morrison*

Opportunities for poking one's head out of a carriage window on a cold winter's day and taking shots like this are almost gone from the main line in these days of automatic doors. No 8770, one of Old Oak Common's numerous '57xx' pannier tanks, is seen at Southall from a passing Paddington-bound express hauling a short trip freight from Old Oak Common to Brentford on 15 February 1952. Built in 1934, No 8770 was withdrawn in December 1962. *Brian Morrison*

No 6016 *King Edward V* weaves its way through the Chilterns near Gerrards Cross with the 4.10pm express from Paddington to Birmingham, Shrewsbury, Chester and Birkenhead, in the summer of 1952. The 'King' had been repainted in BR blue, although it has no indication of ownership on its tender. The leading 70ft-long carriage is also newly repainted, in carmine and cream. No 6016 would be fitted with a double chimney in January 1958 and withdrawn in September 1962. *Brian Morrison*

Southern Region carriages regularly worked over the Western Region's Birmingham main line on through trains to and from the South Coast. Here a rake of Maunsell-designed vehicles forms the 10.10 Birmingham Snow Hill–Margate holiday express, photographed between Seer Green and Gerrards Cross, on Saturday 5 July 1952. The locomotive is No 4924 *Eydon Hall*, of Oxley (84B) depot; built in May 1929, it would be withdrawn in October 1963. *Brian Morrison*

Despite dwindling numbers a 'Star' on top-link duties was still a common sight in the early 1950s, a testimony to the modernity of their design and the appreciation in which they were held by the Operating Department. Indeed, Chief Inspector Pullen of Swindon is quoted as saying: 'Ask any Western Region Shed Superintendent of the time which would be his best "Castle" and he would reply: One of the last-built "Stars"'.No 4061 *Glastonbury Abbey* was one such locomotive, emerging from Swindon Works in May 1922, 15 months before No 4073 *Caerphilly Castle* was completed. It is seen here, operating from its final home, Stafford Road, Wolverhampton, on 5 July 1952, seemingly in effortless charge of a lengthy down Shrewsbury express heading through the lush Chiltern countryside near Beaconsfield. *Brian Morrison*

Although 'Saints' could still sometimes be seen working expresses at this time, the class was very close to extinction, and their principal duties were less demanding. No 2933 *Bibury Court* stands at Shrewsbury station on 28 August 1952 with the 4.50pm all-stations to Birkenhead. It will follow the 4.40pm (the 1.10pm express from Paddington), which beyond Shrewsbury stopped only at Gobowen, Ruabon, Wrexham, Chester and Rock Ferry. At Chester all passenger trains reversed, being usually taken on by a '51xx' 2-6-2T. *Bibury Court* was an 84D Leamington engine and had probably worked up from home earlier in the day on another stopping train. It would be withdrawn four months later, by which time just three of the class would be left, the last survivor being No 2920 *Saint David*, withdrawn in October 1953. However, more than 50 years on a representative of this iconic class, the prototype for the thousands of 4-6-0s which were such a familiar sight in Britain until the very end of steam, is being re-created from a 'Hall' by the Great Western Society at Didcot. *Brian Morrison*

No 7802 *Bradley Manor* gets hold of the 3.10pm train to Pwllheli as it negotiates the sharp curve at the south end of Shrewsbury station on 28 August 1952. *Bradley Manor* was built in January 1938 using parts from a Churchward Mogul. In 1943 the 'Manors', the lightest of all GWR-designed 4-6-0s, were allowed to take up work on the Cambrian section, and throughout the 1950s No 7802 was based at Machynlleth (89C). On the left Collett 0-6-0 No 2234 can be seen backing onto a Severn Valley service, whilst on the right, illustrating that Shrewsbury was very much a joint station, Stanier 'Black Five' 4-6-0 No 44907 is being held in the platform road, awaiting clearance with a southbound goods. *Bradley Manor* can still be seen at work in Shropshire, having been resident on the Severn Valley Railway since 1979. *Brian Morrison*

Amongst the former GWR classes which were not of Swindon origin one of the longest-lived was the Robinson 'ROD' 2-8-0. Here No 3031, of Oxley shed, heads south through Wellington on 30 August 1952 with a long freight bound for Oxley. Robinson, trained at Swindon, was the last CME of the Great Central Railway and might well have been the first CME of the LNER had he not declared himself too old for the post. His powerful 2-8-0s were chosen during World War 1 as a standard design for service with the Royal Engineers in France. Some 521 were built — far more than could be used — and they were sold off extremely cheaply to various railway companies. One hundred were bought by the GWR, at a cost of £1,500 each, but their condition was not good, and in the end the best 50 were given a thorough overhaul. The rest had all gone by the end of 1931, but their tenders lived on, being coupled to 'Aberdares' and '2251' 0-6-0s. The author came across one on the dump at Swindon, with the initials 'ROD' still discernible, in the early 1970s. All but five of the 50 overhauled examples, Nos 3000-49, came into BR ownership, looking far more like something to be encountered on former LNER lines rather than those of the GWR, for there was little obviously 'Swindon' about their appearance. No 3031 would be withdrawn in May 1956, the class becoming extinct in October 1958. *Brian Morrison*

1953

Very few '43xx' Moguls lasted into BR days, nearly all having been converted into 'Granges' or 'Manors' or scrapped. An exception was No 4375, of Stourbridge Junction shed, one of the last four survivors. It is seen here on 11 April 1953 between Denham and West Ruislip hauling a train of coal empties, nearly all of them wooden-bodied, formerly private-owner vehicles — and, like No 4375, soon to disappear. No 4375 was turned out by Swindon in November 1915 and returned there, for the last time, to be broken up in January 1958. *Brian Morrison*

Collett 0-6-0 No 2290, of Worcester shed (85A), crossing the Grand Union Canal south of Denham with a freight for Neasden Yard on 11 April 1953. At the far end of the viaduct is Denham West Junction signalbox. In order to reach Neasden the train will take the former Great Central line at Northholt Junction. The Collett 0-6-0s were just as much at home on branch-line passenger services as they were on goods trains. They were never very common in the London area, Old Oak Common having just three at around this time, although others could be found at Reading and Didcot. No 2290 had been built in 1936 and would be withdrawn in June 1959. *Brian Morrison*

The GWR's treatment of the locomotives absorbed at the time of the Grouping in 1922/3 can best be described as quirky. Some were disposed of — either scrapped or sold — more or less immediately, others were 'Westernised' with GWR-type boilers and other fitments, while yet others were left to carry on much as before, sometimes for several decades, although not always on home territory. The three Midland & South Western Junction Railway 2-4-0s, originally Nos 10-12, fell into the two latter categories. Built by Dübs in 1894, they were rebuilt by the GWR in 1924 and were sent to the Lambourn Valley line and for the next 28-30 years spent their time pottering around the Didcot and Reading areas. No 1336 is seen on home territory at Cirencester Watermoor, 9 May 1953, with a Gloucester Railway Society special. By this date these attractive little engines had outlived all the GWR's own 2-4-0s; indeed, the only other 2-4-0 tender engines still working for British Railways were the ex-Great Eastern Railway 'E4s'. No 1136, the last of the class, was withdrawn in March 1954. *Peter Treloar*

The GWR was probably more addicted to the auto-train than any other of the 'Big Four' and provided a number of different classes to power it. In Edwardian times it had been equally keen on the steam railmotor. This, with the locomotive and the carriage sharing a frame, was not a particularly comfortable means of travel, but the GWR made a better fist of it than most. When the last railmotors disappeared in the 1930s the carriage sections were adapted as auto train trailers. One such is seen here on 8 June 1953, in BR carmine and cream livery (which was supposed to be confined to main-line corridor carriages), being propelled out of High Wycombe towards Banbury by large-wheeled pannier tank No 5424, of Banbury shed. Auto trains were as likely to be found on main lines — especially such as this, which passed through a relatively sparsely populated part of the world — as on branches. No 5424 had been built in 1935, specifically for passenger work, and was withdrawn in April 1959. The '54xx' class had disappeared by October 1963, either displaced by DMUs or else no longer needed on account of branch-line closures. *Brian Morrison*

Our first view of British Railways standard carriages features the 8.37pm Newcastle–Bournemouth West standing at Oxford station on 14 July 1953. Southern Region 'Lord Nelson' 4-6-0 No 30863 *Lord Rodney*, of Eastleigh shed, has just coupled on, hence the driver standing and presumably watching his fireman do the necessary between the tender and the leading carriage. It was perfectly possible to see locomotives from all four pre-nationalisation companies on any normal day at Oxford — various Southern Pacifics, 4-6-0s and, perhaps, Maunsell Moguls on trains to the Hampshire, Sussex or Kent coast, Stanier 2-8-0s on through freights and all manner of ex-LMS and ex-LNER classes working in from Cambridge and Bletchley. Although, not surprisingly, the new BR Mk 1 carriages tended to be used initially on the most prestigious London expresses they also appeared quite early on services such as these. Attached to the two BR Mk 1s is a Maunsell two-coach restaurant-car set dating from the 1920s, while beyond that is a rake of Bulleid corridors. The Southern was always very reluctant to abandon green for its carriages and it soon returned triumphant, BR's carmine and cream being, metaphorically, scraped off. *E.D.Bruton*

Pictured at Yelverton c1953 is No 4410, dating from 1906 and an example of the smallest of all GWR 2-6-2T designs. The train is bound for remote Princetown, on the branch which connected the outside world with Dartmoor Prison, the terminus being 1,373ft above sea level. The '44xx' class had a long association with the branch, which closed in 1956; No 4410 would be among the last three survivors, being withdrawn in August 1955. *Peter Treloar*

1954

'31xx' 2-6-2T No 3102 pulls out of the freight yards north of Wolverhampton on 20 July 1954 with a pick-up goods. There were a number of variations on the large 2-6-2T theme; this one involved taking the frames of a locomotive of the '3150' class (built 1906-8), attaching a new front end and curved platform ends and fitting a new boiler and smaller driving wheels, the intention being to create a new class of banking engine. Only five locomotives were so treated, in 1938/9, and despite their 5ft 3in coupled wheels they were found to be excellent passenger engines. No 3102 was allocated to Stafford Road and could frequently be seen on suburban passenger work in the West Midlands, as well as freight. It was withdrawn in October 1958, the class disappearing altogether at the beginning of 1960. *Brian Morrison*

On 22 July 1954 No 7827 *Lydham Manor* arrives at Shrewsbury from the north with a long, mixed freight originating from Chester. Built by British Railways in December 1950, *Lydham Manor* would be withdrawn in October 1965 but not scrapped, being eventually preserved and restored to running order on the Dart Valley Railway; contrary to rumour it is not true that there are more 'Manors' preserved than were actually built, although it sometimes seems like that. Although up a steep gradient this is in other respects the easiest approach to Shrewsbury, all the other routes involving very sharp curves. Swinging to the right immediately in front of the locomotive is the former LNWR line to Crewe, and it was here that a North–West express came to grief early in the morning of 15 October 1907 when it attempted to take the curve at what the nearby Crewe Bank signalman described as 'over 60mph'. Nineteen people, including both enginemen, died, and a further 31 were badly injured. No satisfactory explanation has ever been offered to explain the driver's lapse.
Brian Morrison

Hayle Viaduct in the summer of 1954. A Churchward '45xx' 2-6-2T is crossing with a westbound freight whilst beneath cyclists are passing in both the up and down directions. Behind the lady with the flowing skirt are parked a motor cycle combination and what looks very like a Morgan three-wheeler, plus two much more modern saloons, an Austin Devon — must have strayed across the border - and a Ford Consul. Hayle, on the St Ives Estuary, has long been a port and became a most important place as the mining industry flourished from the late 18th century. Richard Trevithick had associations with the town. The railway between Hayle and Redruth was opened in 1837, and the viaduct was completed in 1852, although, like so many in Cornwall, it was originally built of wood and later replaced. *Peter Treloar*

1955

'90xx' 4-4-0 No 9017 takes water at Oswestry in August 1955, pausing on its journey from Whitchurch to Welshpool. Oswestry (89A) was 9017's home shed. It had also been the headquarters of the Cambrian Railways, hence the rather grand station building to the left. The '90xx' 4-4-0s were just about the oddest locomotives produced on any UK railway in the 1930s. Weight restrictions precluded any large engines' working the Mid-Wales lines, yet the 'Dukes' which had been the mainstay of most of the passenger work were wearing out, so Swindon simply mounted the top half of a 'Duke' on the bottom half of a 'Bulldog' and, lo and behold, a brand-new outside-frame 4-4-0 which would solve the problem! And it did. Despite the appearance shortly afterwards of Moguls and 'Manors' these antique-looking Victorian survivors had found a niche — one they continued to occupy well into BR days. Indeed, No 9017 lasted until 1960 and was then most fortunately bought by Tom Gomm, who took it to the Bluebell Railway, where it has lived ever since, although in the spring of 2009 it returned to Wales and worked, to great acclaim, for a short period on the Llangollen Railway (see inset). *Author*

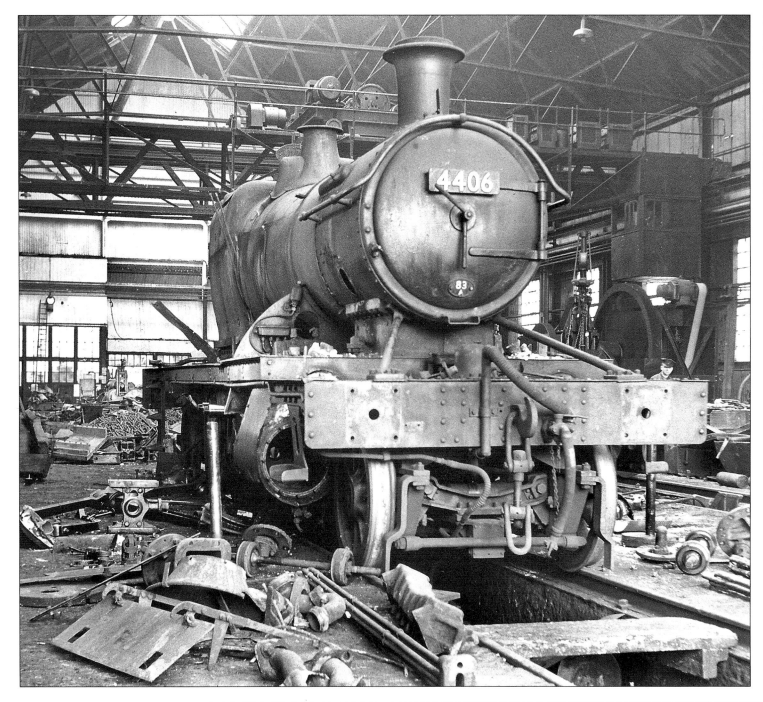

No 4406 under the breaker's hammer at Swindon, 5 November 1955. There were 11 locomotives in the '44xx' class, the smallest variation on the 2-6-2T theme. Built between 1904 and 1906, they proved to be exactly what was needed on the hilly West of England branches. However, the class was never expanded, the slightly larger '45xx' design being preferred, but a 50-year career amply demonstrated just how useful these locomotives were. *Brian Morrison*

1956

No 7007 *Great Western* eases its way past the down-side goods shed at Hereford on a June evening in 1956 to take out the last Worcester and Paddington express of the day, the 6.05pm, timed to arrive in the capital at 10.11pm. This historic locomotive was the very last 'Castle' to be built by the GWR, entering service in July 1946 with the name *Ogmore Castle*. Other 'Castles', of course, followed in BR days, but to mark the disappearance of the longest-lived railway company in the UK No 7007 was renamed in January 1948 and given the GWR coat of arms on the middle splasher. A Worcester locomotive for most of its career, *Great Western* would be withdrawn in February 1963. *Author*

Gloucester on 10 July 1956, with '56xx' No 6631 shunting at the tale end of a ferocious thunderstorm. At its height the author had taken shelter inside the shed, and one particular flash of lightning directly overhead illuminated some dark corners which had probably never before been so exposed! The '56xx' 0-6-2T was Swindon's response to taking over in 1922/3 various Welsh valley railways which had favoured this wheel arrangement. Some 200 were built in a very short time, and whilst they never entirely superseded their predecessors they proved a valuable asset; although they were always associated with South Wales, there was always a number based elsewhere. Gloucester is, of course, within sight of Wales. No 6631 was built in August 1928 and would be withdrawn in September 1963. *Author*

Ruabon, 9 August 1956, with a holiday express about to branch off the main line south to Shrewsbury and head deep into Welsh mountain territory on its way to Barmouth. This was the GWR — as opposed to Cambrian Railways — route through Mid-Wales to the coast. Both had weight restrictions, with the result that double-headed through trains from England were a common sight. In this instance two Croes Newydd locomotives, Collett 0-6-0 No 2209 and Mogul No 7310 are in charge. The train consists of at least 10 carriages, the first a BR Mk 1, the rest of GWR or LMS origin.

By now pre-nationalisation liveries had just about disappeared, the last LMS carriage still in red the author can recall seeing being at Barmouth Junction in August 1954. The route, one of the most picturesque within former GWR territory, will take the train to Llangollen, whence it will run alongside the River Dee, then deep into the mountains by way of Corwen and Bala to Barmouth Junction and across the Mawddach Estuary to its destination. Steam trains can still be found running between Llangollen and Carrog. *Brian Morrison*

Looe station in 1956, the terminus of one of the most picturesque of all the Cornish branches, reached at the end of the deep, wooded East Looe River valley from Liskeard. The branch-line station at Liskeard is situated at a right-angle to its main-line counterpart, and branch trains take a long curve through 180° before passing under the main line and continuing down into the valley to Coombe Junction, where they end up facing the direction from which they started; they then reverse down the valley to Looe. Beyond Coombe the line once again passes under the main line to reach Moorswater, where there is a cement terminal; there was also a small locomotive shed, which closed when the line was 'dieselised' on 11 September 1961. The 'B' set seen here is hauled by 2-6-2T No 4568, built in October 1924 and destined to be withdrawn in February 1959. *Peter Treloar*

Inset: Looe harbour, January 2010. *Author*

Ex-Taff Vale 0-6-2T No 364 high on the moors at Hirwaun on the line from Neath to Aberdare in December 1956. It is hauling the Cardiff Valleys Inspection saloon, a Dean clerestory, hence the gentlemen in trilby hats giving the track the once over. On the far right is 2-8-0T No 4252. The line closed in 1964. Built in 1916, No 364 was one of 58 examples of the 'A' class, the most numerous and newest Taff Vale design, all of which reboilered by the GWR, having originally been poor steamers. In rebuilt form they were excellent locomotives, used on passenger and goods work. No 364 was among the last survivors, being withdrawn in March 1957, and by the end of that year the class had disappeared entirely. *Peter Treloar*

The station at Nantymoel, deep in its Welsh valley, in December 1956. Terminus of a GWR-built branch, it closed in 1958. Pictured in charge of two carriages forming a Bridgend train, '57xx' pannier tank No 9660 had been built in 1948 and would be withdrawn in November 1964.
Peter Treloar

Wreathed in smoke and steam, a '56xx' 0-6-2T pauses at Ebbw Vale (Low Level) on a bleak December day in 1956; a sprinkling of snow lies on the empty platform. The terminus of a typical valleys branch from Newport, the station closed to passenger traffic in 1962. The vast steelworks continued to provide plenty of freight activity but eventually went out of business and by early 2008 the site had been virtually levelled. However, somewhat remarkably a combination of funding from various bodies was to see a revival of the branch: a new terminus was built at Ebbw Vale Parkway, south of the original, and passenger trains once again ran from 6 February 2008. A free bus connection was provided into the town centre, but sadly a lack of funding saw its withdrawal in the summer of 2009. *Peter Treloar*

In a Welsh valley opposite a row of terraced houses on a wet December day in 1956, there is no mistaking that this is an auto-train, hauled by '4575' 2-6-2T No 4580, of Cardiff Cathays depot. The station is Senghenydd, one of the saddest places in Britain, for on 14 October 1913 there occurred here the greatest pit disaster ever to befall a Welsh mining community: an explosion in the colliery killed 436 miners, leaving 205 widows and 542 fatherless children. An earlier disaster, in 1901, had seen the death of 81 miners. The colliery, opened in 1877, closed in 1928, the line, built by the Rhymney Railway, in 1964. No 4580 was built in 1927 and withdrawn in June 1958. *Peter Treloar*

1957

No 9401, of Old Oak Common depot, shunts at Bethnal Green, on the Eastern Region main line out of Liverpool Street, alongside a former Great Eastern 'J69' 0-6-0T No 68596, February 1957. Transfer freights regularly took Western Region locomotives across London to the other Regions, both north and south of the river. The presence of the electric overhead, seen here, resulted in warning flashes' being affixed to locomotives and tenders which were likely to work beneath them, although electrification would not come to the London area in the Western Region until decades later, when the line to Heathrow was opened. No 9401 was one of just 10 of its class built by the GWR (the only ones fitted with superheaters), the rest coming out under BR; the final example, No 3409, was completed by the Yorkshire Engine Co as late as October 1956. No 9401 would be withdrawn in July 1963. *R. C. Riley*

'Modified Hall' No 6960 *Raveningham Hall* accelerates away from Hereford past Rotherwas Junction, where the Gloucester line diverged, on 28 August 1957 with a North–West express comprising a typical mix of 11 ex-GWR and ex-LMS carriages. Second of the 'Modified Halls', built in March 1944, No 6960 would be withdrawn in June 1964 and sent to Woodham's yard at Barry. From here it was rescued and restored in time to take part in the 150th-anniversary celebrations of the Stockton & Darlington Railway at Shildon in 1975. Later it worked on the Severn Valley, Gloucestershire-Warwickshire and West Somerset railways. *Author*

Inset: The preserved No 6960 at Bridgnorth, on the Severn Valley Railway, pictured in the spring of 1990. *Author*

A Cardiff-bound train accelerates way from Gloucester on 11 September 1957. This was the original main line from London to South Wales before the Severn Tunnel, at the time of its construction the longest rail tunnel in the world, was completed in September 1885. The locomotive is No 4980 *Wrottesley Hall*, of St Philip's Marsh depot, Bristol (82B), the first carriage the final Hawksworth design of bow-ended, sloping-roof Brake Third; next is a slightly older Third, followed by a bow-ended Composite dating from the 1920s. Built at Swindon in February 1930, *Wrottesley Hall* would be withdrawn in July 1963. *Author*

'51xx' 2-6-2T No 4145, of Newton Abbot, accelerates away from Dawlish station in November 1957 with the Kingswear portion of 'The Cornishman' — four chocolate-and-cream Mk 1s, a Brake Composite, a Composite, a Second and a Brake Second. The 'Cornishman' left Wolverhampton at 9.15am - 'seats can be reserved in advance of a fee of 1s 0d' — and arrived at Exeter St Davids at 2.8pm. Here the train divided; the main portion, usually 'Castle'-hauled, continued to Penzance, whilst one of the big 2-6-2Ts would take charge of the Kingswear portion, calling at Dawlish at 2.42pm, Torquay at 3.19pm and Paignton 3.28pm, before reaching its destination at 3.50pm. Completed at Swindon in September 1946, No 4145 would be withdrawn in December 1962. *Author*

1958 — STEAM STILL ASCENDANT

As 1958 dawned in many ways the Western was still the Great Western Region. A visitor to Paddington would have found 'Kings' and 'Castles' in charge of nearly all the long-distance expresses, backed up by the 'Halls'; suburban trains were the almost exclusive preserve of the '61xx' 2-6-2Ts, whilst pannier tanks were the favoured motive power for the long lines of empty carriages arriving from or departing to the carriage depot at Old Oak Common. The one intruder on the main line scene was the 'Britannia' Pacific. Although Churchward had produced Britain's first Pacific, *The Great Bear* of 1908, the Great Western had found the 4-6-0 capable of dealing with the heaviest and fastest expresses, although rumour has it that in the 1940s F. W. Hawksworth, the company's last CME and a man who had worked with Churchward, had in hand designs for a 4-6-2. British Railways' first standard design had come from the former LMS works at Crewe, and although much of the thinking here had, ever since the arrival of Stanier from Swindon in the early 1930s, reflected Churchward ideals, the new Pacifics looked very much in the LMS tradition. Officially mixed-traffic locomotives, they were given a power rating of 7, rather than the 8 of the 'Kings', the Stanier Pacifics, the LNER-designed 'A1s' and 'A4s' and some A2s and the Southern 'Merchant Navies'.

Eight of the original 25 'Britannias' had been allocated in 1951 to the Western Region — to Old Oak Common, Newton Abbot and Plymouth Laira sheds — but later gravitated to Cardiff Canton, where the crews seemed happy enough to work them. Nevertheless these handsome locomotives were not universally welcomed. Some of this could certainly be put down to the conservative attitude of ex-Great Western crews. O. S. Nock had footplate rides on a number of them in the autumn of 1951 and remarked that 'the locomotives concerned performed well, particularly No 70019 *Lightning*, on the up "Cornish Riviera" between Penzance and Plymouth and No 70022 *Tornado*, between Newton Abbot and Plymouth'. Nevertheless, there was a feeling that a Pacific was not the ideal wheel arrangement for the steep gradients west of Newton Abbot and that if something more powerful than a 'King' were contemplated (which the 'Britannias' did not claim to be) a 4-8-0 might be the answer. The standard '4MT' 4-6-0s could be found on the Cambrian coast, as could the little '2MT' 2-6-0s, and a few of the '5MT' 4-6-0s also appeared on the Western Region. BR-design '3MT' 2-6-2Ts worked in limited numbers alongside GWR locomotives of the same wheel arrangement but never supplanted them. There seemed to be no need for the Western to employ the big Riddles 2-6-4Ts, appreciated as they were elsewhere, but the very fine '9F' 2-10-0s impressed Western crews, along with all others. Generally, however, GWR-design locomotives maintained their pre-eminence. The larger mixed-traffic 4-6-0s — including the 'Counties', which, whatever their official designation, were no more mixed-traffic locomotives than were the 'Kings' or 'Castles' — had been restored to lined green livery (something the 'Granges' and 'Manors' had never worn when GWR property), emphasising the individuality of the Western Region. Very soon even some pannier tanks would emerge from overhaul at Swindon in lined green, as would the Standard 4-6-0s.

Rather more in evidence were the BR Standard-design carriages — the Mk 1s, as they came to be known. These were to be seen on most of the principal expresses, exclusively in many cases, although quite a number of GWR-design carriages

Super saloon No 9118 at Old Oak Common in 1960.

including the Super Saloons and restaurant cars, including some going back to Edwardian times and rebuilt in the late 1930s or '40s, were still on front-line duties. Chocolate and cream was back in a big way, a modified version of the GWR colours being applied to named expresses, of which there had recently been a considerable proliferation. Clerestory carriages were all gone, other than those in departmental use, as were nearly all 'toplights', although one or two still appeared regularly at Paddington on the Channel Islands boat train to Weymouth and Newbury race specials. All carriages not reserved for the named expresses were being repainted in an approximation of LMS maroon, whilst the surviving diesel railcars received the same shade of green as that applied to newly delivered BR DMUs.

The 'Toad' goods brake van, with its big open balcony, was still a familiar sight bringing up the rear of all manner of goods trains and was also in departmental service, but the BR design of brake van, basically of pure LNER origin, was commonplace. Another distinctive vehicle was the 'Siphon G' bogie milk van, production of which had been continued for some years by British Railways but which was now much used as a parcels van and was in this respect like the 'Fruit D' long wheelbase six-wheel van which found favour with British Railways.

Although the Modernisation Plan of 1955 had sounded the death-knell for steam, at the beginning of 1958 the Western Region had just one main-line diesel locomotive, this being No D600, a rather clumsy-looking diesel-hydraulic built by the North British Locomotive Co and powered by a pair of German MAN 1,000hp engines. There were plenty of 350hp shunters (the '08s', as they would become and can still be seen in some numbers today), whilst the first diesel multiple-units — very much a development of the GWR's AEC railcars — had appeared on the Western in 1957.

The 'Kings' were still the principal motive power on the West of England main line between Paddington and Plymouth, and between Paddington and Wolverhampton. Redesigning the front end and the fitting of double chimneys had been going on and would soon be complete. Swindon had gone on building 'Castles' until 1951 and the class totalled 166, withdrawals of some of the rebuilds from 'Stars' having taken place. The fitting of double

chimneys to the 'Castle' class had also begun, in May 1956, the first two being No 4090 *Dorchester Castle* and No 7018 *Dryslwyn Castle*. From the same month double chimneys were also fitted to the 'Counties' (a process completed in October 1959), which class probably benefited most of all from this innovation. By contrast the last 'Star', No 4056 *Princess Margaret*, had been withdrawn in October 1957 (No 4003 *Lode Star* being already preserved), while the last 'Saint', No 2920 *Saint David*, had gone in October 1953.

All the 'Granges' were still at work, although no more had been built, but a final 10 'Manors', Nos 7820-9, had been turned out in 1950, which year also saw construction of the final 'Modified Halls', the last being No 7929 *Wyke Hall*, completed in November.

All of Churchward's '28xx' 2-8-0s and their Collett successors remained at work, although withdrawal of the Churchward locomotives would begin in 1958. The '47xx' continued to work heavy overnight goods trains whilst enjoying something of an Indian summer on passenger trains, appearances on weekend West of England expresses becoming quite common in the summer months. But if you wanted to be sure of seeing a Churchward-era locomotive still on express work in summer, then his 'Mogul' was the best bet. Although withdrawals of the '43xx' series and their conversion into 'Granges' and 'Manors' had been very nearly complete by 1939, two — Nos 4358 and 4377 — were still around in 1958, the former, remarkably, adorned in lined green. A number of the '53xx' series had been withdrawn, as had just two '63xx' (Nos 6321/83) in 1956. All the original '73xx' locomotives remained, as did the Collett '93xx' versions, although these were in the process of being modified to work over weight-restricted routes and consequently were being renumbered into the '73xx' series.

All the 'Dukes', 'Bulldogs' and 'Dean Goods' had gone, although of the latter No 2516 was preserved. Despite the advent in Central

Above: The restored *Lode Star*, hidden from the public in the Stock Shed at Swindon on 15 July 1959. Ahead is the as yet unrestored Dean Goods No 2516.

Below: Exeter Corporation buses of the period.

Above: One of the most popular motobikes of the time.

Below: By the late 1950s despite traffic jams around Exeter, long-distance coaches were providing increasing competition for the railways.

Wales of firstly Churchward Moguls, then 'Manors' and finally BR Standard '4MT' 4-6-0s, not all the remarkably antique-looking outside-frame '90xx' 4-4-0s had been withdrawn, eight still being at work. Most extraordinary was the re-emergence of a long withdrawn 4-4-0, *City of Truro*, which had come out of preservation to work specials but was also employed on ordinary passenger duties, notably on commuter trains between Oxford and Paddington. All the Collett '2251' 0-6-0s were still at work.

Inevitably heavy inroads had been made into the locomotives inherited from the Welsh companies in 1922/3, so that those numbered below 1000 were down to single figures, three being the Vale of Rheidol narrow-gauge 2-6-2Ts, two more the stored narrow-gauge Welshpool & Llanfair 0-6-0Ts. There were, however, a few other inherited Welsh locomotives numbered above 1000. Of the native GWR types the last of the once numerous '2021' pannier tanks, dating from the late 1890s, had been withdrawn in 1957, but two of the even older '850' class, Nos 2008 of 1892 and 2012 of 1894, remained, the very last tank engines of the Dean era.

All 11 of the short-wheelbase, outside-cylinder '1361' and '1366' tank engines were still in existence, but what would strike even the most casual observer when surveying Western Region pannier tanks in 1958 was the huge number that had been built following nationalisation. Just 10 of the taper-boilered '94xx' had been built by the GWR, but no fewer than 200 had emerged under BR auspices, the last, No 3409, as late as October 1956 — well into the era of BR Standard construction and some time after the Modernisation Plan of 1955 had declared that the days of steam were numbered. Then there were two brand-new classes, the '16xx' (effectively modernised '2021s'), 70 of which were built between 1949 and 1955, and the 10 '15xx' of 1949, a real break with tradition in that they had outside cylinders, taper boilers and Walschaerts valve gear. Twenty more '74xx' were built in the years 1948-50, whilst 41 of the standard '57xx' class were built between April 1948 and

December 1950. The construction of 321 pannier tanks for British Railways, when it was obvious that the diesel shunter, albeit with a limited top speed, could perform most of their duties far more effectively, was just one example of the many money-wasting indulgences perpetrated by the nationalised railway system.

Turning to the 2-6-2Ts we find that the entire '44xx' class had been withdrawn, and that 39 of the '45xx' dating from 1906-13 had gone, that 30 of the Churchward '3150s' had been withdrawn (leaving just three still at work) and that three of the five '31xx' had gone, as had just one of the '81xx' class (No 8105). Of the larger Collett tanks four of the '51xx' class had been withdrawn, but, as yet, none of the '61xx'. No 2-8-0Ts had been withdrawn since 1948, and the '72xx' class of 2-8-2Ts remained intact.

Withdrawal of the '14xx' 0-4-2Ts had begun — not surprisingly as branch lines closed and DMUs appeared — but there were still nearly 60 in stock, whilst the total of non-auto-fitted '58xx' had been reduced by around a half, to 10.

Of the GWR diesel railcars, 12 had been withdrawn.

Clearly, much of the old Great Western remained in 1958, but if enthusiasts were lulled into thinking that, because not much had disappeared in the preceding 10 years, not a lot would go in the next decade, they could not have been more wrong. Indeed, 1958 would see main-line diesels entering service; the following year the first 'Castles' proper (as opposed to rebuilt 'Stars') would be withdrawn, as would the first 'Halls', and by 1960 the withdrawal of GWR-built locomotives was gathering ominous momentum. Branch lines were also being closed, and this, together with the arrival of many more DMUs, meant that many classes of smaller locomotives, particularly tank engines, were being decimated. It has to be said that the DMU was largely welcomed by the general public, being faster, cleaner and often (though not always) more comfortable than the steam-hauled carriages it replaced. The replacement of steam on the main line was inevitable, for in the full-employment years of the 1950s and '60s it was almost impossible to recruit sufficient men to work in the dirty and sometimes dangerous conditions of the locomotive shed and on the footplate, allied with the unsocial hours raising steam and maintaining it demanded. Whether the early main-line diesels represented a sound investment is another issue altogether.

1958

No 3845, an example of Collett's '2884' development of the Churchward's '28xx' 2-8-0 design, heads through Evesham in March 1958 with a train of empty iron-ore wagons bound for Banbury from South Wales. A resident of Oxley (84B) shed, No 3845 had been completed during World War 2, in April 1942, and would be withdrawn in June 1964. *Peter Treloar*

The author took considerable pleasure in recording this picture on 4 April 1958, for a beautifully polished lined-green '61xx', with express headlamps, hauling eight Collett corridor carriages, all in carmine-and-cream livery, made a stirring spectacle. The '61xx' 2-6-2Ts were, of course, just about the commonest locomotives seen in the London area, generally doing what they were designed to do, which was haul rakes of non-corridor carriages between Paddington, Reading, Oxford and the various Thames Valley branches. No 6158 had been completed in March 1933 and would be withdrawn in June 1964. *Author*

Left: The Helston branch in the spring of 1958. Churchward '45xx' 2-6-2T No 4563 is watched by two lads lurking in the long grass between Truthall Halt and Nancegollan as it hauls its train of Hawksworth- and Collett-era non-corridor carriages towards Gwinear Road. *Peter Treloar*

Below: Abingdon station in 1958, with 0-4-2T No 5818 standing at the terminus of this short branch from Radley, on the Didcot–Oxford main line. The branch closed to passenger traffic in 1965 but remained open for freight, one of its customers being the MG car factory in Abingdon. The picture is somewhat deceptive, for the 0-4-2T, despite being attached to an Hawksworth auto-train trailer, is

not, in fact, working as an auto-train, for, unlike the otherwise identical '14xx' 0-4-2Ts, the '58xx' were not equipped for such work. Indeed, one wonders how much use these 20 small, four-coupled locomotives, built as late as 1933, really were: No 5818 was withdrawn in September 1959, and the class was extinct by April 1961, more than four years before the last auto-fitted '14xx' was taken out of service. Your author regrets never travelling the Abingdon branch, for although stationed at RAF Abingdon in 1956 he always took the rather more convenient bus to either Radley or Oxford. *Peter Treloar*

The low midsummer sun, shining across the Bristol Channel and the Somerset Levels shortly after 9pm on the longest day of the year in June 1958, highlights the undersides of '61xx' No 6137 and its long train of corridor carriages of GWR origin (aside from the 1920s-vintage LMS-built open Brake Second, leading), as it speeds past Yatton, heading back probably with day-trippers from Weston-super-Mare to Bristol. Although primarily London-area locomotives the '61xx' Prairie tanks could be found elsewhere, No 6137 being at this time a resident of St Philip's Marsh; built in October 1932, it was, however, destined to end its career at Stourbridge, in November 1964. *Author*

One of the outside-cylinder, short-wheelbase '1366'-class pannier tanks, introduced in 1934 for precisely this sort of work, has charge of a trainload of fruit and vegetables from the Channel Islands as it heads along Weymouth Quay towards the Town station and goods yard on 17 July 1958. Such traffic once provided much revenue for the railway. Passenger boat trains, transferred to the Southern Waterloo route, continued well into the diesel era, providing much entertainment as road traffic increased and cars, parked illegally, had to be manhandled out of the path of trains. The scene on the water, as well as alongside it, has changed greatly, hundreds of pleasure craft now being moored in the marina. *Peter Treloar*

Not quite the 'Cornish Riviera' as one might expect it. Although the date is 26 July 1958 the carriages of the Western Region's most famous named express, in a mixture of crimson-lake and carmine-and-cream liveries, all pre-date nationalisation, some being the best part of 30 years old, whilst motive power is provided by two Churchward-design '45xx' tank engines, the leading one, No 4547, being 44 years old, the other, No 4573, a mere 34. But this is a summer Saturday, and the train has started from St Ives rather than Penzance, the usual rake of chocolate and cream BR Mk 1 carriages forming, in effect, a relief. *Peter Treloar*

'WD' 2-8-0 No 90365 takes the through line at Oxford with an up freight in the summer of 1958. A number of these heavy-freight locomotives were allocated to the Western Region, although this one was at the time based at Market Harborough, on the Midland main line of the London Midland Region. Designed during World War 2 by R. A. Riddles, who later became British Railways' one and only CME, they were almost the equivalent of the American 'Liberty Ships', being of basically well-tried design, built rapidly and simple to maintain, but not very comfortable and not intended for a long career. Shunned both by cleaners and the enthusiast fraternity, the 733 'WDs 2-8-0s were actually rather handsome locomotives, with simple, uncluttered lines, and lasted until almost the end of steam on BR. *Peter Treloar*

Left: A development of the 'WD' 2-10-0 was Riddles' '9F' 2-10-0. Arriving as they did right at the end of the steam era on the railways of Britain (the last one, No 92220 *Evening Star*, completed at Swindon in 1960, being BR's very last main-line steam locomotive), the 251 locomotives of this class scarcely had time to show their worth. Their premature withdrawal not only represented a terrible waste of motive power that could easily have served for another 20 years; it was also a tragedy, for in their short lives they proved themselves to be truly exceptional locomotives, immensely powerful yet remarkably free-running and well capable of taking over passenger trains when required and running with them at speeds in excess of 80mph — in effect the spiritual successors of the GWR '47xx' 2-8-0s. No 92187 is seen here under construction at Swindon in 1958.
Peter Treloar

Right: Nice pair of braces. Two spectators wonder just what was the attraction of photographing Dovey Junction in the rain; now they know. 'Small Prairie' No 4560 arrives on 4 August 1958 with the 09.30 Barmouth– Machynlleth; completed in September 1924, it would be withdrawn in August 1959.
Brian Morrison

We met No 4980 *Wrottesley Hall* in 1950 at Tyseley and in 1957 in charge of a Gloucester–Cardiff train. This time it is seen leaving Stratford-upon-Avon on 15 August 1958, with the 10.35am Paignton–Wolverhampton express. Looped to let it pass is a goods train hauled by 'Large Prairie' No 5163, of Tyseley (84E) depot, although as Stratford-upon-Avon was a sub-shed of Tyseley it could well be a local engine. Built in November 1930, No 5163 would be withdrawn in November 1959. *Brian Morrison*

Ex-Swansea Harbour Trust 0-4-0ST No 1142 shunts at Clee Hill Summit on 15 August 1958. This branch line left the North & West main line just north of Ludlow, which has a strong claim to being the loveliest town in England. In contrast Clee Hill, at 1,814ft, is 'bleak, treeless and shaped by decades of quarrying' (*Shropshire*, a Robert Hale County Book), and, despite appearances to the contrary on this sunny summer afternoon, is often in winter wreathed in fog, giving it and its many derelict buildings a ghostly air. The line closed in 1960, but the trackbed and the ruins of the loading structure are still in evidence, and quarrying, which at one time employed some 2,000 workers, who came by train from Ludlow, Bridgnorth, Cleobury Mortimer, Worcester and elsewhere in the surrounding district, continues. No 1142, built by Hudswell Clarke in 1911, was withdrawn in November 1959. *Brian Morrison*

Inset: A view from Clee Hill on a summer evening in 2009, looking south towards the Shropshire/Herefordshire border. *Author*

There is something very odd about this picture, taken at Leamington Spa 16 August 1958, for the train is the 9.10am cross-country service from Margate to Wolverhampton, and one might expect it to be made up of GWR- or Southern-design carriages, or even LMS. But, no, the Mogul, No 6346, is hauling a long rake of ex LNER carriages, three of the first four being Thompsons, the other a Gresley Brake

Second. But then this is a summer Saturday, and just about anything was possible on such a day; it was around this time that the author witnessed an 'N2' bringing a rake of green Maunsell carriages into King's Cross to form a Newcastle extra! No 6346 had been built in April 1923 and would be withdrawn in September 1964. *Brian Morrison*

City of Truro about to enter Old Oak Common shed on a wet September morning in 1958. This famous locomotive had been removed from York Railway Museum at the beginning of 1957 and sent to Swindon, where it was carefully (of course) restored to working order, the restoration including a replacement boiler — one of the benefits of GWR standardisation. It then appeared at all sorts of celebrations but, uniquely among restored locomotives from the National Collection, was used in between in revenue-earning service, being based at Didcot. One such duty involved the 7.30am Reading-Paddington commuter train and 6.20pm return, hence the locomotive's appearance here at Old Oak Common. *Author*

Below: *City of Truro* at Didcot with a contemporary clerestory coach in 2007. *Author*

Shrewsbury shed, 13 September 1958. From left to right: No1017 *County of Hereford*, No 4037 *South Wales Borderers* and No 1013 *County of Dorset*. The 'County' class was in the process of being modified with double chimneys which No 1017 would receive in March 1959, No 1013 had been so equiped eight months earlier. The 'Counties' did excellent work on the North to West main line between Shrewsbury and Bristol and South Wales, Shrewsbury shed being allocated six of the class at this time. No 1013 was built in February 1946 and No 1017 a month later. No 1017 was withdrawn at the end of 1962; No 1013 was one of the last three last survivors, being taken out of service in July 1964. No 4037 was one of the most most remarkable express passengers engines ever to run in the United Kingdom on account of its longevity. Completed at Swindon as a 'Star' class locomotive, *Queen Philippa*, in December 1910, it was rebuilt as a 'Castle' in June 1926 but containing many of the original parts and would have been considered on many other railways as the same engine, albeit somewhat altered. The most instantly noticeable difference were the larger boiler and the window cab. A number of 'Star' class engines became 'Castles' but No 4037 outlived them all and was not withdrawn until September 1962 surviving, albeit by a few months, many of the locomotives built from scratch as 'Castles'. In its working career of 51 years and 9 months No 4037 covered 2,429,722 miles, almost all of it on top link duties, a record not only for a GWR engine but possibly for any British locomotive. *Author*

The GWR was particularly keen on auto-trains, and BR's Western Region continued to build Hawksworth design auto-trailers. Here 0-4-2T No 1424 has charge of 1930s-vintage Collett and BR Hawksworth design trailers as it leaves Gloucester on 27 September 1958 with the 13.10 to Kemble.

On the left a couple of tender engines are awaiting calls to duty, prominent being No 7312, one of the later Churchward Moguls dating from December 1921, freshly overhauled and resplendent in lined green livery. Nos 1424 and 7312 would both be withdrawn in December 1963. *Author*

The scene at Gloucester shed on 27 September 1958. Churchward Mogul No 5382 stands on the turntable of its home shed under the critical eye of its driver as other railwaymen go about their business in the background. The author doubts whether he had official permission to be there, but in a less security-conscious age an obviously genuine enthusiast, particularly one with a camera, could usually wander around a steam shed unchallenged. One of 10 GWR Moguls based at Gloucester at this time, No 5382 had been built in June 1920 and would be withdrawn in April 1959, seven months after the photograph was taken. *Author*

1959

Having paused at Fowey station, the driver of 0-6-0PT No 7446 has a brief chat with the stationmaster before moving onto the Up Goods line in March 1959, probably during the course of shunting at the china clay loading wharf at nearby Carne Point. Fowey station would close to passenger traffic in 1965. The line from St Blazey is no more, having being converted into a private road to bring lorry loads of china clay from Par to Fowey for export, but that from Lostwithiel remains open for bulk loads of clay from the pits around St. Austell, such as the one pictured below. No 7446 had been built in March 1950 and would be withdrawn in July 1964. *The Rev Hedley Sparks*

Above: One of the best-known locations on Britain's railway network. Photographed from one of the rearmost carriages, the 'Castle'-hauled 'Cornish Riviera' crosses the Tamar on Brunel's magnificent Royal Albert Bridge as it leaves Cornwall for England — as some Cornishmen would have it — in April 1959. Off-camera to the right is the great naval base of Devonport, while on the far bank, passing beneath the approach spans of the bridge, is the former LSWR main line from Plymouth to Exeter. *Peter Treloar*

Right: No 6000 *King George V* looks highly regal simmering away in the spring sunshine on 5 May 1959 at Old Oak Common depot before being turned and backed down to Paddington to take out a West of England express. *Author*

In the spring of 1959 '57xx' pannier tank No 3732, of Wellington depot — situated just across the platform whence it is making such a vigorous exit — has charge of the 5.50pm train to Much Wenlock, which consists of two bow-ended corridors dating back to the 1920s. Corridor carriages were a common enough sight on such workings, although the Wellington–Crewe line tended to favour non-corridor stock, as did the LMR-worked trains from Shrewsbury to Wellington and Stafford.

At one time the line to Much Wenlock continued through deeply rural Shropshire to join the main Hereford–Shrewsbury line at Marsh Farm Junction, north of Craven Arms, but this section closed in 1951, and the remainder was to follow suit in 1962. No 3732 had been built in 1935 and would be withdrawn in May 1962. *Brian Morrison*

The Western Region's pride and joy, the 'Bristolian', British Railways' fastest train, eases past Subway Junction, dead on time, on 3 June 1959, a few days before steam gave way to 'Warship' diesel-hydraulics. The locomotive is No 5085 *Evesham Abbey*, of Bath Road shed; This had begun life in December 1922 as 'Star' No 4065, and although it re-emerged as a 'Castle' as late as July 1939 it was a genuine rebuild, retaining many 'Star' parts. Thus by the time of the photograph it was nearly 37 years old, yet it could still be entrusted with this most prestigious of workings. The train is made up of six BR Mk 1s and a late GWR dining car, all resplendent in chocolate and cream. *Evesham Abbey* would be one of the last single-chimney 'Castles' to be withdrawn, in February 1964. *Author*

'14xx' 0-4-2T No 1420 pulls out of Culmstock on 30 July 1959 with the 1.40pm Tiverton Junction-Hemyock. Opened in May 1876 as the Culm Valley Light Railway, this 7¼-mile branch, worked on the 'one engine in steam' principle, was to close in 1963. The carriage is a former Barry Railway brake third. No 1420 would be withdrawn in November 1964 and immediately purchased for preservation on the Dart Valley Railway (nowadays known as the South Devon Railway). *Peter Treloar*

High summer in the far West. At 10.30 on the morning of 5 August 1959 the Wolverhampton-bound 'Cornishman' pulls out of Penzance, its rake of chocolate-and-cream BR Mk 1 carriages hauled by No 7022 *Hereford Castle*. Alongside, '94xx' pannier tank No 8473 is shunting stock for the next departure, which will leave for Paddington at 11am. Built in June 1949, No 7022 had been fitted with a double chimney in January 1958 and would be withdrawn in June 1965 along with No 7034 *Ince Castle*, leaving No 7029 *Clun Castle* as the sole surviving active member of the class. No 8473, meanwhile, would be withdrawn in January 1961. *Peter Treloar*

Below: Something seems to be amiss at Banbury on Saturday 8 August 1959. A signalman is standing between the up and down through platform lines holding a red flag as No 6008 *King James II* waits for the road with the 11.45am Birkenhead–Paddington express. Two tracks over is passenger pannier tank No 6413, which had a regular turn powering auto-trains between Banbury and High Wycombe, while beyond can be seen a pair of horseboxes. Banbury station had only recently been completely rebuilt and is little changed today, even retaining semaphore signals. This was the last full year of steam monopoly on the Birmingham main line, 'Western' diesel-hydraulics arriving in 1962, in which year the entire 'King' class would be withdrawn, No 6008, completed at Swindon in March 1928, being among the first to succumb, in June. No 6413, built in 1932, would be withdrawn in November 1961. *Author*

Right: Immaculate 'County' No 1008 *County of Cardigan* stands ready to depart Penzance with the up 'The Cornishman' on 9 September 1959. Built in December 1945, it would be withdrawn in October 1963. *Peter Treloar*

Hauled by Churchward 2-8-0 No 2845, of Newport (Ebbw Junction) shed, a goods train from South Wales, with high-sided wooden coal wagons prominent, eases its way past Coleham sheds, Shrewsbury, on 14 September 1959. The flexible nature of the old wagons when filled with coal reminds one of the bow which used to develop in wooden-bodied carriages after several decades of service, although two of the three wagons nearest the camera look almost pristine in their coat of freshly applied grey paint. The coal wagons in the shed yard seem to be almost exclusively steel-bodied. In the foreground (left) is a '94xx' 0-6-0PT engaged in shunting duties. *Author*

The down 'Cornish Riviera' takes the through road at Exeter St Davids on 26 September 1959, passing '4575' 2-6-2T No 5524 on a stopping train for Paignton. Despite being double-headed by 'Modified Hall' No 6995 *Benthall Hall* and North British diesel-hydraulic No D601 *Ark Royal* the 'Riviera' is running three-quarters of an hour late. No doubt *Ark Royal* set out from Paddington with the best of intentions but somewhere along the route must have suffered a major setback, requiring the assistance of the 'Hall', a Taunton resident. The five A1A-A1A 'Warships' foisted on the Western Region represented one of the biggest wastes of money in which British Railways indulged in the early days of 'dieselisation'; no more powerful than a 'Castle' but infinitely less reliable and grossly overweight, they were a nail in the coffin of the once great North British Locomotive Co and had very short lives, barely outlasting the likes of *Benthall Hall*, built by British Railways in December 1948 and destined to be withdrawn in March 1965, right at the end of WR steam. *Peter Treloar*

1960

A spotless No 4566 leaving St Erth on 14 April 1960 with the 11am to St Ives. The first two carriages are Collett bow-ended corridors. A Penzance locomotive, No 4566 had been built in October 1924 and would be withdrawn in April 1962. However, this was far from the end of its story, for it had the good fortune to be sent to Dai Woodham's yard at Barry, where it languished for many years before eventually being rescued and restored to working order on the Severn Valley Railway. *Peter Treloar*

Inset: Another preserved member of the class No 4561 when on display at STEAM — Museum of the Great Western Railway, at Swindon. *Author*

The up 'Royal Duchy' crosses Angarrack Viaduct on 14 April 1960 behind 'Warship' diesel-hydraulic No D815 *Druid*, with No 6824 *Ashley Grange* piloting and seemingly doing plenty of work. Introduced in 1959 and based on a German design, the Swindon-built B-B 'Warships' were elegant-looking machines but not particularly reliable, especially in the early days, which might explain why *Druid* required assistance from a locomotive built more than two decades earlier, in January 1937 (and destined to be withdrawn four years after the photograph was taken). The 'Royal Duchy', leaving Penzance at 11.30am, making 11 stops in Cornwall before reaching Plymouth North Road at 2.30pm and then stopping six more times before reaching Paddington at 7.30pm, was hardly a flier; the 'Cornish Riviera', making fewer stops, was 40 minutes quicker between Penzance and Plymouth and a further 35 minutes quicker over the remainder of the journey to Paddington. *Peter Treloar*

Pannier tanks were a familiar sight at Paddington almost until the end of steam, hauling empty stock in and out. Old Oak Common had a batch of '97xx' fitted with condensing gear so that they could take themselves down into the depths of the Underground and reach Smithfield meat market, and it was thus not surprising to come across one of them. However, No 9707, recorded at lunchtime on 18 April 1960, is otherwise employed, rather appropriately passing over the District Line tracks at Subway Junction as it approaches the terminus, at little more than walking pace, with its train of crimson-lake Mk 1s. *Author*

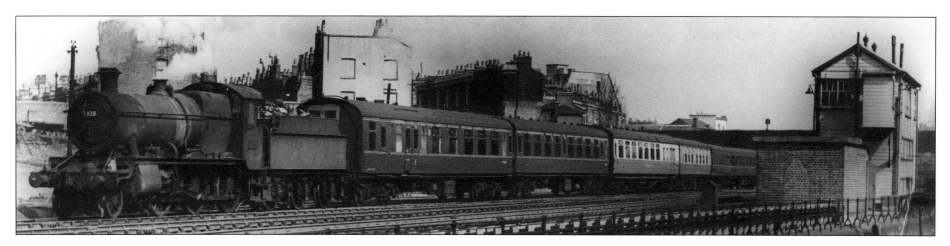

Passing Westbourne Park on 18 April 1960, Collett Mogul No 7328 heads away from Paddington with the empty stock from a recently arrived express. Until 1958 numbered 9306, this locomotive had been completed in March 1932 and was destined to be withdrawn from Severn Tunnel Junction shed 30 years and one month later in April 1962, having covered 911,837 miles. The carriage formation, a mix of crimson lake and carmine-and-cream, is typical of the time, comprising a Mk 1 Brake Composite, a Mk 1 corridor Second, a rebuilt 70ft Churchward restaurant car, a Mk 1 open First (some of the tables no doubt being laid for dining) and two Hawksworth carriages. *Author*

'Granges' were never a common sight in the London area, but here we have two for the price of one, Nos 6834 *Dummer Grange* and 6854 *Roundhill Grange* being seen passing Subway Junction on 3 June 1960. The former is from Taunton shed, the latter from Oxford. This was not the first time the author had seen a 'Grange' hauling this train (which unfortunately was not recorded), an early-evening departure from Paddington made up of GWR-design carriages. *Dummer Grange*, completed in August 1937, would be withdrawn in June 1964; *Roundhill Grange*, turned out in November 1937, was destined for withdrawal in October 1965, that year seeing the end of the surviving 45 examples of this class of mixed-traffic locomotive. *Author*

When it was announced in 1955 that steam was to be phased out by BR and that diesel and electric traction would soon become universal, production of one of the most successful British steam designs of all time had only just begun. Derived from Riddles' own 2-10-0 design of World War 2, the '9F' not only proved to be ideal for hauling the heaviest freight trains but it also showed a remarkable turn of speed and was often used on passenger trains, particularly on holiday extras at weekends and over the hilly, curving Somerset & Dorset route between Bath and Bournemouth. The very last steam locomotive to be built for British Railways was '9F' No 92220, which emerged from Swindon in 1960 and to mark the occasion was turned out in lined passenger green and named *Evening Star*, in traditional GWR style. It was allocated to Cardiff Canton shed, where the Western Region's 'Britannias' had made their home. On the morning of 27 June 1960, the Pacific diagrammed for the 'Red Dragon' failed, and, perhaps tongue in cheek, the shedmaster substituted No 92220, seen here following an on-time arrival at Paddington. In the ensuing three weeks the 2-10-0 worked this prestigious express on several more occasions, always keeping time, until a higher authority stepped in. Later transferred to the Somerset & Dorset, *Evening Star* had a woefully short BR career of just five years before passing into preservation and resuming work on the main line for a while. When the author travelled behind it the crew advised that it had reached 83mph, adding that they could not be certain that all the wheels were touching the rails all the time! In the summer of 2010 *Evening Star* was on display, appropriately, at STEAM — Museum of the Great Western Railway in Swindon, where it was built (see left). *Author*

The view south at Hereford on 6 July 1960. Coming off shed in the foreground is pannier tank No 1662 (built by BR as recently as March 1955 and destined to be withdrawn, after a career of less than nine years, in December 1963), while on the opposite side of the tracks is Barton goods depot. The main line here was normally used only by goods or any Abergavenny-bound passenger trains not stopping at Hereford station — which all passenger trains normally did. In the distance was Red Hill Junction, where the line from the station joined the goods line, while behind the photographer was the junction with the former Midland Railway branch to Credenhill, Hay-on-Wye and Three Cocks Junction. Remote from the rest of the Midland network, the line was destined to close in 1962. *The Rev Hedley Sparks*

Chester General station, 8 July 1960. The GWR liked to use the term 'General' instead of 'Central' for large stations and presumably neither the LNWR, nor its successor, the LMS, objected. A picture which perfectly encapsulates the joint nature of the establishment where rival Euston- and Paddington-bound expresses met, albeit facing opposite directions. Hughes/Fowler 'Crab' 2-6-0, No 42856 is arriving with an express from the Crewe direction, the leading carriage looking very like a Collett design bow-ender. Alongside is No 44738, one of the less-than-standard LMS 'Black Fives', this one, fitted with Caprotti valve gear, dating from 1948 and therefore of BR origin. On the far side is November 1920-built Churchward 2-6-0 No 5399 with a very shiny smokebox which would indicate it has just received works attention, probably for the last time; by now its days were numbered, withdrawal taking effect in September 1962. *The Rev Hedley Sparks*

Aberystwyth station on 12 July 1960. Standard '2MT' 2-6-0 No 78000 is departing with the 5.15pm to Pwllheli, the leading carriage a late-1930s brake composite, still in red and cream livery. There are a number of other locomotives in steam in the distance and in front of the shed including, on the right beside the water tower, a 'Manor' with the 'Cambrian Express' headboard and highly polished front buffers. *The Rev Hedley Sparks*

Johnston, 13 July 1960. '57xx' 0-6-0PT No 3639 stands in the station with the 2.20pm from Milford Haven, whilst in the distance the 2.30pm from Neyland to Paddington is pulling in behind No 1020 *County of Monmouth*. No 3639 was built in October 1939 and withdrawn in January 1963. The 'County', a Neyland locomotive, had been built in December 1946 and would be withdrawn in February 1964. *The Rev Hedley Sparks*

Inset: Milford Haven station earlier the same day, with No 3639 in the distance prior to taking the 2.20pm to Johnston. Although Milford Haven is still served by rail, unlike Neyland, this site is now occupied by the inevitable retail outlets. *The Rev Hedley Sparks*

Maesycwmmer & Hengoed, 13 July 1960. This was the view from Hengoed Viaduct towards the station as the 7.38pm, consisting of a Collett 'B' set and a Hawksworth non-corridor Second and hauled by one of the original '57xx' 0-6-0PTs, departs for Newport. Built by the Brecon & Merthyr Tydfil Junction Railway, Maesycwmmer & Hengoed was closed in 1962. Hengoed Low Level station, built by the Rhymney Railway, still exists. Hengoed Viaduct, completed in 1858 as part of the Taff Vale Extension Railway, is now a Grade 2* listed structure and part of a cycle path from Quakers Yard to Newport (see inset). *The Rev Hedley Sparks*

MORRIS MINI-MINORS
More Mini-magic!
NOW WITH HYDROLASTIC® SUSPENSION

Hinksey, down side, 1960 — a vastly busy yard, as can be seen, flanked by the main line from Didcot to Oxford and the Hinksey River. Collett '2884' 2-8-0 No 3857, which has obviously had some attention paid to its smokebox (hence the shine) waits to depart, whilst standing alongside is another mixed freight, its load including at least three new Minis, built at the nearby Cowley works. No 3857 was built in October 1942 and would be withdrawn in March 1964. *Peter Treloar*

Afon Wen, on the shores of Tremadoc Bay, in the summer of 1960. This was where the former LNWR line from Menai Bridge and Caernarvon met the former Cambrian Railways line to Pwellheli. In this view it appears to be well supplied with water tanks and signals but somewhat lacking in prospective passengers or trains, although Fairburn LMS-design 2-6-4T No 42674 can be seen at rest in the distance on the far left. *The Rev Hedley Sparks*

The view north at Oxford station in the summer of 1960. A 'Hall' 4-6-0, rather unusually paired with a 3,500gal tender with capacity for 5½ tons of coal, stands at the head of a stopping train; beyond is a '57xx' 0-6-0PT, while in the distance is the locomotive shed. On the right is the former LNWR station, the iron pillars of which were constructed by the same firm that built the Crystal Palace, and of a similar design; this has now been re-erected at the Buckinghamshire Railway Centre at Quainton Road. *The Rev Hedley Sparks*

Inset: The Bodleian Library, Oxford. *Author*

1961

No 7019 *Fowey Castle*, one of the post-nationalisation locomotives dating from May 1949, storms past Subway Junction with a Newbury race special on 4 March 1961. This was the last year in which such specials, hauled by highly polished locomotives, were made up of GWR-design carriages, mostly First-class and with lavish dining accommodation; note the two-car Collett restaurant-car set, fourth and fifth in the formation. Much the most interesting carriage is the leading one, No 8179. A magnificent 70ft-long 'toplight' Brake First, it was completed in September 1910 for the Fishguard boat train; one of the very few unrebuilt 'toplights' to be repainted in lined maroon and one of the very last in ordinary service (First No 8324 being probably the only other survivor by this time), it would be withdrawn later in 1961. *Fowey Castle*, an Old Oak Common locomotive, had gained its double chimney in September 1958 and would remain in traffic until February 1965, only Nos 7022, 7029 and 7034 outlasting it in BR service. *Author*

Inset: Preserved 'toplight' saloon No 9055, photographed in 2008 at Kidderminster, on the Severn Valley Railway. *Author*

The Western's pride and joy, No 6000 *King George V*, heads past Old Oak Common on 4 March 1961 with the 3.10pm Paddington–Birkenhead express, which on this occasion seems to be unusually lightly loaded, comprising just seven Mk 1s. By now the 'Kings' had been replaced on the West of England main line by diesels and were concentrated on South Wales expresses and particularly the main line to the north by way of Birmingham, on which they had been unchallenged for more than 30 years. All this would come to an end with the withdrawal of the entire class by December 1962. *King George V* was chosen to represent the class in preservation and was originally stored at Swindon. *Author*

Inset: Following the final 'fifteen-guinea' run of August 1968 from Liverpool to Manchester and Preston and back to Liverpool steam disappeared entirely from the BR network, but intense lobbying eventually resulted in a rescinding of the ban, and in September 1971 *King George V*, by now in the care of H. P. Bulmer Ltd, the Hereford-based cider maker, made a triumphant return to the main line, hauling a train of restored Pullmans, seen arriving at Old Oak Common from Birmingham prior to being displayed at Kensington Olympia. *Author*

The up 'The Red Dragon' in the Thames Valley on 10 March 1961 on its way from Carmarthen to Paddington, hauled by a Swansea Landore (87E) single-chimney 'Castle'. Departure from Carmarthen was at 7.15am; in all, 12 stops were made in South Wales, the last, at Newport, at 10.20am, following which the train ran non-stop to Paddington, arriving at 12.55pm. The return journey began at 5.55pm, Carmarthen being reached 10 minutes before midnight. 'The Red Dragon' was one of many of the many Western Region expresses which took advantage of the edict that such trains could sport chocolate-and-cream livery — although bright red might have been more appropriate! *Author*

Two horses graze oblivious to No 6009 *King Charles II* climbing into the Chilterns with the 7.25am Pwllheli-Paddington on a warm June day in 1961. The nine carriages are all of pre-nationalisation origin, retained for just such a summer extra, but will, like the locomotive, soon be no more. Photographed from the bridge carrying the GWR London-Birmingham main line — the 1910 cut-off route via High Wycombe and Bicester — over the original route via Reading and Oxford, the train is on the up line, which will come together with the down line high on a lengthy embankment upon which Aynho Park station was precariously placed. North of Bicester there was nothing like the local traffic there is today — just four up trains on weekdays, none on Sundays. Aynho Park closed in 1963. Below it on the Oxford line was Aynho for Deddington, a more substantial edifice set beside the Oxford Canal, but not much busier. It closed in 1964, but its buildings remain. *Author*

Although the 'Large Prairie' tanks regularly worked portions of expresses in the West Country and South Wales they could be seen at summer weekends on express duties on almost any part of the system. On Saturday 24 June 1961 Banbury's No 5167 appears to be making light work of the 10-coach 10.25am Poole–Bradford as it speeds past Aynho towards Deddington. The first two carriages are ex-LMS, the next is a former LNER Gresley buffet car, while the rest are BR Mk 1s. An hour-and-a-half earlier No 5167 had gone past with a stopping train bound for Oxford, where it presumably took over the express from a Southern Region locomotive; at Banbury it would hand over to an Eastern Region engine. *Author*

The 'South Wales Pullman' gathers speed as it passes Subway Junction behind 'Castle' No 5051 *Earl Bathurst* on 5 July 1961. The GWR availed itself less of the Pullman option than did any of the other 'Big Four' companies, and although the Western Region was rather more inclined to dip its toe into the Pullman world, notably with the 'Blue Pullman' diesel units, the 'South Wales Pullman' was the only such train to be regularly steam-hauled. The up train left Swansea High Street at 6.40am, calling at Port Talbot, Bridgend, Cardiff and Newport, arriving at Paddington at 10.15, and returned from Paddington at 4.55pm, reaching Swansea at 8.40pm. The supplementary charge in one of the Second-class cars, such as those seen here at the head of the train, for the entire one-way journey was 5s 6d (27$\frac{1}{2}$p); First class was 10s 6d (52$\frac{1}{2}$p). 'Meals and refreshments [were] served at every seat, but 'dogs, motor scooters, perambulators, etc [were] not conveyed'. No 5051 was completed at Swindon in May 1936 and named *Drysllwyn Castle*, but it was reported that certain of the aristocracy whose names had been bestowed on the humble '32xx' (later '90xx') 4-4-0s were unimpressed by this perceived indignity, so the names were transferred to 'Castles'. No 5051, a Cardiff Canton resident, was withdrawn in May 1963 but was rescued from Woodham's scrapyard at Barry, restored at Didcot and has since often been seen back on the main line, bearing both names at different times. *Author*

Inset: No 5051 at Didcot in 2007. *Author*

Left: Churchward 2-8-0 No 4705 approaches Reading from the Bristol direction on a sunny Saturday evening in July 1961 with a train of empty stock. Despite the widespread takeover of much main line passenger work by 'Warship' diesels and the withdrawal of many 'Castles' and 'Halls' it was remarkable how often the mixed-traffic 2-8-0s turned up at this time on passenger work, especially at weekends. 'Indian summer' may be an overworked term, but it precisely describes the situation applying to these handsome locomotives at this time, and this year in particular. Withdrawals were about to begin, and No 4705, having covered 1,656,564 miles since completion in April 1922 — more than any other member of the class — would be taken out of service in December 1963. Equally under threat was the stock it is hauling, one Stanier-period LMS corridor carriage and eight of GWR origin. Rakes of pre-BR carriages were retained at this time for extra summer traffic, but this practice was about to come to an end. *Author*

Below: 'Britannia' No 70016 *Ariel* passing Subway Junction with an express from South Wales on Saturday 12 August 1961. This carriages must have been hauled out from some Welsh siding, and this would surely have been their last summer before being sent off to the scrapyard, for all are of prewar origin. The majority are Collett 'bow-enders' dating from the 1920s, but the second vehicle is a 1930s ex-LMS Brake Composite, whilst the sixth is an older, 1920s Fowler-era former LMS Third. *Ariel* — what a splendid name for an express locomotive — has had its smoke-deflector hand-rails replaced by hand grips, following the fatal accident involving 'Britannia' No 70026 *Polar Star* near Didcot in 1955. *Author*

The 'Cambrian Coast Express' arriving at Shrewsbury on 14 September 1961. It was only at this late date that 'Kings' worked right through to Shrewsbury, instead of coming off at Wolverhampton. No 6013 *King Henry VIII*, of Old Oak Common, was by the time of its withdrawal nine months later the most-travelled of all the class, in its 34-year career having covered all but two million miles (1,950,462, to be precise), just about all of it on top-link duties, which must constitute some sort of record. For some reason it is without nameboard and has its train-reporting number chalked, albeit quite neatly, on its smokebox front. The first carriage is a strengthening 'bow-ender' dating, like the locomotive, from the 1920s; the rest are chocolate-and-cream BR Mk 1s. In the siding are two passenger brake vans, the 'bow-ender' being labelled to work between Paddington and Penzance and between Paddington and Shrewsbury. *Author*

1962

Right at the end of their careers the surviving GWR-design railcars were painted green, the same shade as applied to BR-designed DMUs and railcars. These were direct descendants of the GWR vehicles, which were far and away the most successful of the various pre-nationalisation attempts to stem passenger decline on the branch lines, although they also operated certain main-line services. No W29W, one of the later examples, delivered in the years 1940-2, survived until 1962, their final year of operation. It is seen here heading out of Shrewsbury for Bridgnorth and has just passed Coleham locomotive sheds. This year also witnessed the closure of the line between Shrewsbury and Bridgnorth and on to Kidderminster and Worcester, although the southern section would later be revived as the celebrated Severn Valley Railway and would see identical preserved railcar No 22 operate on a couple of occasions from its home at Didcot (see inset). *Author*

1963

The 'Manors' continued to be mainstay of through trains from London and the West Midlands to the Welsh coast well into the 1960s. In this August 1963 picture No 7808 *Cookham Manor* is seen on Talerddig Bank with an up express. The leading carriage is a prewar LMS-built Brake Second, followed by a Collett 'bow-ender', a Hawksworth and then a BR Mk 1. *Cookham Manor* had been built at Swindon in 1938; upon withdrawal in December 1965 it was immediately bought by a member of the Great Western Society and from 1966 was often seen working specials out on the main line — an almost seamless passing from one role to another. *P. H. Wells*

Inset: *Cookham Manor* on its way to Shildon in 1975 with the Great Western Society's train of preserved GWR-design carriages. *Charles Whetmath*

A '9F' doing precisely what it was designed for. With steam to spare, No 92107 approaches Solihull station, on the Birmingham-Paddington main line, hauling a long rake of empty iron ore wagons on 19 May 1964. *Michael Mensing*

1965

The very last ordinary scheduled steam departure from Paddington was the 16.15 to Banbury on 11 June 1965, for which No 7029 *Clun Castle* was the chosen motive power. In this series of pictures taken at Subway Junction we see it first of all backing down towards the terminus and passing a 'Western' diesel-hydraulic on a South Wales express and then heading out in charge of its train of dark-red-painted BR Mk 1 and LMS-design corridor carriages. Not surprisingly, the train was packed with a great many enthusiasts as well as ordinary passengers. No 7029 was the very last 'Castle' in ordinary service and remained employed until the end of the year, passing into preservation at Tyseley, whence it continued to appear on the main line. The locomotive continues to be based at Tyseley, where at the time of writing it is awaiting overhaul. *Author*

Above: Southall depot, 14 June 1965. The last shed in the London area whence steam still operated is host to a grimy '9F' and the soon-to-be-preserved No 6106. Although there had long been a depot here that seen here dated only from early BR days, having been completed in 1953. It was destined to close six months after this picture was taken but remains *in situ* today. Southall has a special place in the preservation movement, for it was here in 1964 that four grammar-school boys who used to watch trains from the footbridge leading to the shed decided that one of the '14xx' 0-4-2Ts which worked auto-trains from Southall should be preserved; thus began what is now the Great Western Society, with its unique collection of just about everything appertaining to the GWR. *Author*

Right: The scene at Gloucester shed one Saturday in June 1965, featuring a grimy, unidentified 'Grange' (its name and numberplates removed, either for safe keeping or stolen), '57xx' 0-6-0PT No 9672 and Brush Type 4 (Class 47) No D1583. *Author*

Steam survived on the Cambrian main line from Shrewsbury through Welshpool to the coast until 1966, and amongst the last active GW-design 4-6-0s were Shrewsbury's 'Manors', which remained working until 1965. No 7828, officially *Odney Manor* but by now minus its nameplates, approaches the junction with the line from Hereford on its way to Shrewsbury with the up 'Cambrian Coast Express' in the summer of 1965. The leading carriage is a BR-built Hawksworth, the rest being BR Mk 1s, all in dark-red livery, the chocolate-and-cream which once distinguished WR expresses having been abandoned. Built in December 1950, No 7828 is one of a remarkable number of 'Manors' that were rescued over the years from Dai Woodham's scrapyard at Barry and, restored to working order, is based nowadays on the West Somerset Railway. *Author*

Inset: *Odney Manor* at Llangollen in 1990. *Author*

Shrewsbury (Coleham) shed in the summer of 1965. On the far left is a BR '4MT' 4-6-0, next to it a toplight carriage in departmental use, while beyond are another '4MT', two 'Manors' and a 'WD' 2-8-0. The shed here was originally a joint establishment, this side having been built by the LNWR; by now the adjoining Great Western premises were used as a home for DMUs. *Author*

Miss Susan Butler, perhaps not surprisingly, turns away from grimy LMS-design Fairburn '4MT' 2-6-4T No 42104 as it climbs the steep bank out of Birkenhead Woodside and passes Birkenhead depot (where a Hughes/Fowler 'Crab' 2-6-0 is just visible) with a Paddington express in the summer of 1965. Regular steam haulage south of Wolverhampton had ended in September 1962, former GWR lines north of Aynho Junction passed to the London Midland Region in September 1963, and any remaining GWR-design locomotives at Birkenhead and Chester disappeared. Many Paddington trains were diesel-hauled south of Chester, and in March 1967 the through Birkenhead–Paddington service was withdrawn. *Author*

Around Wrexham was an extensive network of lines serving collieries, and Croes Newydd shed was still home to GWR locomotives after steam working on the Western Region had officially ceased, for by then it had been transferred to the London Midland Region and consequently would not close until March 1967. There was always plenty of work for pannier tanks, 11 being based there in early BR days. Here, on 5 October 1965, No 9630 has charge of the early-morning Wrexham-Minera goods, seen passing Brymbo East Crossing. This locomotive would remain in service until September 1966, by which time it was one of the last pannier tanks still at work on BR. *J. K. Norbury*

Challow station, once used by John Betjeman, on 13 November 1965. Today there are no stations still open between Didcot and Swindon, and the HSTs roar happily by, unimpeded, at 125mph. Although demolition has just begun the pagoda waiting room, a quirky architectural feature unique to the GWR, is still intact on the up platform, as are the neat main station buildings beyond the bridge, plus the goods depot and sidings in the distance with a former auto-train trailer in departmental service parked in front, while the signalbox is just visible at the end of the down platform.
The Rev Hedley Sparks

Inset: The reason The Rev Hedley Sparks was at Challow that day — to photograph No 4472 *Flying Scotsman*, then in the ownership of Alan Pegler, passing with a private train in collaboration with the World Wildlife Fund, the 'Panda Pullman'. This was scheduled to operate from Paddington to Cardiff in 140 minutes, in fact arriving three minutes early — a steam record for that run.
The Rev Hedley Sparks

1966 AND BEYOND

The last scheduled Western Region shed to operate steam was Banbury, which cleared out its remaining locomotives in the autumn of 1966. There had been some steam-hauled freight workings on the Bristol to Birmingham main line until August, and what was termed the last official passenger working was by No 7029 *Clun Castle*, which by then must have been used to performing last rites, on a special from Paddington to Bristol and Gloucester on 27 November 1965. This locomotive had worked the final scheduled steam turn from Paddington, the 4.15 to Banbury, on 11 June 1965, hauling a train of BR Mk 1 and LMS-design carriages — a bit of an insult, given that some GWR-designed coaches were still around and could have been rostered. A short while later a '61xx' pulled in with empty stock. Old Oak Common shed had closed to steam, but Southall, long home to a large fleet of '61xx' 2-6-2Ts, was still open. What is generally believed to be the very last scheduled Western Region passenger train, on 3 January 1966, was hauled to Oxford by No 6998 *Burton Agnes Hall*, which was immediately bought by the Great Western Society from Oxford shed; she was just 17 years old, in early middle age by the standards of a decade earlier. The very last standard-gauge GWR-design locomotive to be withdrawn by BR from ordinary service would appear to have been, fittingly, '57xx' pannier tank No 4646, which worked at Croes Newydd shed, by then in the London Midland Region, until November 1966.

Like steam locomotives, GWR-designed carriages were being removed from service and broken up with indecent haste. One uses the description 'indecent', not out of a misguided sense of nostalgia but simply on economic grounds, for the last Hawksworth-design carriages were only 11 years old and could easily have served as long again. But if the excellent '9F' 2-10-0s, some scarcely run in, were being removed from BR's books, along with many other far-from-time-expired BR Standard locomotives (not to mention the various pannier tanks built in the 1950s and the 'Castles' and 'Counties' which had only recently gained double chimneys and thus a new lease of life), what chance did they stand? It has to be said that France and Germany managed the end of steam rather better than did British Railways, and within the British Isles Northern Ireland found a role for its Derby-designed 2-6-4Ts into the 1970s. There were, however, other countries, notably the USA, which dispensed with steam just as rapidly as Britain, and with equal lack of common sense.

The 'Kings' were all taken out of service in a single year, 1962 — a uniquely abrupt slaughter of a region's top-link motive power, but it at least meant that they were never relegated from express passenger duties. Their mantle passed to the 'Western'class diesel-hydraulics, which, rather like the East Coast 'Deltics' as successors of the legendary 'A4s', almost instantly acquired a following of their own, for they were possibly the most handsome of all the big diesels; however, this

Left: Aberayron. By the end of the 1960s so many former GWR branch line stations looked like this. *The Rev Hedley Sparks*

Above: No 823 Countess on the Welshpool & Llanfair Railway in 2009.

Below: Shannon at Didcot during the GW150 celebrations of 1985

Below right: For a while the diesel-hydraulic era still depended on steam-age technology as here at the entrance to Old Oak Common loco and carriage depots.

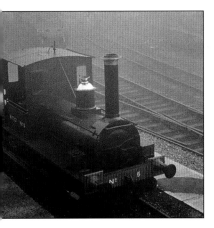

would not save them from the eagle eye of the accountant, who deemed them inefficient in comparison with diesel-electrics, and none served anything like the 30-plus years of the 'Kings', although they did cover comparable (or greater) mileages.

A 'King', No 6000, the pioneer 'Castle', No 4073, a Churchward 2-8-0, No 2818, the pioneer '94xx' pannier tank, the last 'Dean Goods', No 2516, and diesel railcar No 4 were preserved as part of the National Collection, joining 'Star' No 4003 *Lode Star*, whilst *Tiny* (the only surviving broad-gauge locomotive), Wantage Tramway 0 4-0WT *Shannon* and, of course *City of Truro*, were already preserved, as was a replica of the broad-gauge 2-2-2 *North Star* which was built in 1935 to commemorate the GWR's centenary but included parts of the original (although no one seems to know precisely how many). This was not a bad representation, being a lot better than that of most other railways, although, of course, there were many omissions, which all had their advocates.

However, there was a source which, as 1968, the final year of scheduled main-line steam on British Rail, receded into the past, would fill many of the omissions and result in the GWR steam era being represented far more comprehensively than that of any other railway, probably in the world, certainly of comparable size. As scrapping of steam locomotives accelerated in the 1960s — there were 2,846 of GWR design still on BR's books on 1 January 1960, 14,452 in all — Swindon's and other works' capacities to deal with it was stretched beyond their limits, and a number of outside contractors were engaged. Woodham Bros, of Barry, received its first locomotives — Churchward 2-6-0s Nos 5312/60/92/7 — for scrapping in 1959, and by 1968 the total had reached 163. There were also 125 of BR, SR, LMS and LNER design. Cutting up duly began, but as Woodhams concentrated its efforts on wagons the number of locomotives grew, and soon appeals were being launched with the aim of rescuing some of these locomotives — the very first for Churchward

2-6-0 No 5322, which left for Caerphilly where it was restored by the South Wales Group of the Great Western Society and returned to steam in December 1970. The yard closed in November 1989, by which time 98 GWR-design locomotives had been rescued.

Meanwhile a number of '57xx' pannier tanks were bought by London Transport for engineering duties, and when these were eventually disposed of in June 1971 several passed into preservation, as did some pannier tanks sold earlier for industrial work. Other locomotives, not already recorded, which passed straight from BR ownership into preservation were 'Castles' No 4079 *Pendennis Castle* and double-chimney No 7029 *Clun Castle*, 'Manor' No 7808 *Cookham Manor*, '9xxx' 4-4-0 No 9017, '2251' 0-6-0 No 3205, '45xx' 2-6-2T No 4555, '61xx' 2-6-2T No 6106, '14xx' 0-4-2Ts Nos 1420/42/50/66, '56xx' 0-6-2T No 6697, 0-6-0PTs Nos 1369 and 1638, 0-6-0ST No 1363, 0-4-0ST No 1338 and the two Welshpool & Llanfair 0-6-0Ts, Nos 822/3. Nor should not it be overlooked that, following the end of regular main-line steam, there remained in active service the three Vale of Rheidol narrow gauge ex-GWR 2 6 2Ts, which alone upheld steam working throughout the BR era.

1966

Woodham's scrapyard at Barry became a last home (or so it was thought at the time) for many steam locomotives. The first to arrive were four GWR Moguls, in March 1959, many more followed, a number were cut up, but by the end of BR steam in August 1968 some 217 were still there. Western and Southern Region classes predominated. Because Dai Woodham postponed the breaking up of many of the locomotives for year upon year, most were eventually bought for preservation, some long since restored to working order, others still rusting hulks. The first appeal to be launched to rescue a Woodham's locomotive focused on Churchward 2-6-0, No 5322, now at Didcot, although this was not actually the first to leave the Barry yard. In this scene a '42xx' 2-8-0T (left) is being attended to, some parts presumably being removed for another preservation project; also in view are a 'Standard' 2-6-4T, a '2MT' 2-6-2T, two '4575' 2-6-2Ts, a Collett 2-8-0 and a great many Bulleid Pacifics.
Frank Dumbleton

Below: Croes Newydd shed was to remain open to steam until the spring of 1967, and although it had been transferred to the London Midland Region some GWR built locomotives survived into 1966, after the Western Region had officially totally abandoned steam. In this 1966 view a '2251' 0-6-0 stands abandoned, its numberplates removed, whilst in the distance is a BR Standard '4MT' 4-6-0. *Author*

Above: Birkenhead shed. The Western Region presence at what had been a joint LMS/GWR depot gradually declined in the early 1960s, following the LMR takeover. From the winter of 1962/3 some 50 '9F' 2-10-0s were based here, chiefly for hauling trains to and from the John Summers steel works, on the banks of the River Dee at Shotton (at one time the preserve of Robinson Great Central 2-8-0s), as well as for Birkenhead Docks traffic. The last '9F' would be taken out of service in October 1967, when the shed closed. *Author*

1968

August 1968 is the date usually quoted for the end of normal steam working on British Rail, when the final 'fifteen-guinea' run was made by LMS-design Stanier 'Black Five' 4-6-0s and BR 'Britannia' Pacific No 70013 *Oliver Cromwell*. But this was not so. Far to the west, in the mountains of Mid Wales, three 2-6-2Ts (a wheel arrangement particular popular with Swindon) and a fleet of Swindon-designed carriages remained at work on the Vale of Rheidol Light Railway. The gauge was 1ft 11½in, the line running 11¾ miles from Aberystwyth to Devil's Bridge. One of the 2-6-2Ts, No 9, was built by Davies & Metcalfe of Manchester in 1902. The other two were built at Swindon to a virtually identical design in

1923. The following year No 9 was given a heavy rebuild; in effect a brand-new engine emerged, being labelled a 'rebuild' for accounting purposes. In this picture No 7 *Owain Glyndwr* is seen at the head of a rake of GWR-built carriages, their similarity to Collett main-line corridor stock, notwithstanding certain narrow-gauge characteristics, being most marked.
The Rev Hedley Sparks

Inset: No 9 in BR blue livery in the early 1970s. *Author*